Post-Literacy and Continuing Education

POST-LITERACY AND CONTINUING EDUCATION

P. ADINARAYANA REDDY
Asst. Director,
Dept. of Adult Education,
S. V. University, Tirupati. (A.P.)

Discovery Publishing House
New Delhi- 1100 02

First Published-1999
Reprint: 2011

ISBN 81-7141-433-8

Published by:
Discovery Publishing House
4831/24, Ansari Road, Prahlad Street,
Daryaganj, New Delhi-110 002 (*INDIA*)
Phone: 3279245
Fax: 91-11-3253475

Printed at:
Dynamic Printers,Delhi

PREFACE

The experience in the field of adult education in India shows that in the absence of a learning environment and effective programmes of continuing education, the efforts made in literacy programmes yield extremely limited results. Recognising this, the New Education Policy clearly warrented for institutionallisation of scheme of Jana Shikshana Nilayam (JSN) was conceived (1988) and implemented through out the country. The role of JSN is multidimensional and is intended for overall development of the individual and the community was a whole. In order to study the functioning of the programme formulated, relevant data was collected, analysed and the findings were presented.

The present report consists of five chapters. Chapter-I briefly describes the genesis of the scheme of Jana Shikshana Nilayam, Objectives, Functions, Clienitle, Roles the preraks and review of related research. The Statement of problem, scope and need of the study, objective, hypotheses, variables incorporated and limitations of the study is presented in the second the various tools used and steps involved in development of the same, locale of the study, size of the sample and findings and discussion of the study in five sections. Section I describes the infrastructural facilities available, timings and users of the JSN. The extent of the performance of the various roles of the JSNs are presented in the Section II. Section III illustrates the profile of working preraks, influence of the personal characteristics of preraks, influence of the personal characteristics of preraks on their effectiveness and the characteristics of an effective prerak. Section IV presents the reading interests of the neo-literates and the literature supplied to the JSNs. The last section of the chapter analyse the factors associated with the functioning of the JSNs. The summary and conclusions forms the last chapter of the book.

I express my deep sense of gratitude to the Indian Council for Social Science Research, New Delhi for providing adequate financial assitance for conducting this study, without which present investigation could not have been possible.

I am also thankful to Sri. G. Reddeppa, Sri. G. Ramana Reddy, Sri. B. Janardhana Rao, Research Scholars of the Dept. of Adult Education, S. V. University, Tirupati for their assistance in collection of data.

Finally, I am greatly obliged to the field functionaries of adult education in Rayalaseema Region of Andhra Pradesh for their co-operation and assistance in collection of data. Further I am also greatful to all preraks, neo-literates and community representatives who have served as subjects of the study.

Dr. P. A. Reddy

CONTENTS

1

INTRODUCTION

Viewing Adult Education as a means for reducing the economic, social and gender disparities, the Government of India has launched the National Literacy Mission (NLM) in 1988 as one of the five Technology Missions. The NLM aims at imparting functional literacy to 100 million non-literate persons in the age group of 15-35 years by the end of 1997. The NLM assumes that literacy is an indispensable component of human resource development and an essential tool for communication, learning and for sharing of knowledge and information. Hence it has laid emphasis on skill development, creation of awareness among the learners about the national goals of development programmes and for liberation from oppression. Earlier, the National Policy on Education (1986) also stressed on the following items.

(i) Re-organisation of the existing programme to introduce flexibility and other measures for greater effectiveness.

(ii) Application of Science & Technology and Pedagogical Research for improving the pace and environment of learning.

(iii) Establishing linkage between adult education and the developmental programmes.

(iv) Launching of Mass Functional Literacy Programme.

(v) A multi-demential programme of continuing education as the instrument for moving towards a learning society.

(vi) Creation of dynamic management structures to cope with the targets envisaged.

(vii) A distinct slant in favour of women's equality and taking of all measures in pursuance of this resolve.

However, the experiences in the field of Adult Education shows that in the absence of learning environment and effective programme of post-literacy and Continuing Education Programmes, the efforts made in eradication of illiteracy yielded an extremely limited results. Keeping this in view, the National Policy on Education rightly stressed that continuing Education is an indispensable aspect of the strategy of Human Resource Development and the goal of creation of a learning society. Continuing Education includes post-literacy for neo-literates and school drop-outs for retention of literacy skills, continuation of learning beyond elementary literacy and application of this learning for improving their living conditions. It has also stressed for institutionalisation of the post-literacy and continuing education on permanent basis.

Keeping the recommendations of the National Policy on Education (1986) the Government of India evolved a Scheme of Post Literacy and Continuing Education popularly known as Jana Shikshana Nilayam (JSN) in 1988. Since then JSNS were established and were functioning all over the country for the promotion of literacy among the new literates. Each JSN covers a cluster of 4-5 villages with a population of about five thousands. Each JSN will be manned by a functionary known as prerak.

1. OBJECTIVES OF THE JANA SHIKSHANA NILAYAM

The objectives of the JSN as envisaged by the scheme were

i. Provision of facilities for retention, continuing education and application of functional literacy.

ii. Dissemination of information on development programmes, widening and improving participation of traditionally deprived sections of society.

iii. Creation of awareness about national concerns such as national integration, conservation and improvement of the environment, women's equality, observance of small family norms, etc. and sharing of common problems of the community.

iv. **Improvement of economic condition and the general well-being as well as improvement of productivity.**

v. Recreation and healthy living.

The above objectives of JSN clearly indicates that it has to perform a number of specific functions for the promotion of literacy, creation of awareness and improvement of skills.

2. FUNCTIONS OF THE JANA SHIKSHANA NILAYAM

As per the scheme of JSN, the functions of the JSN were as follows

i. **AN EVENING CLASS** : For upgradation of literacy and numeracy skills to be organised for 3-4 hours once a week. The learners would have the option to come for about an hour at any time convenient to them on that day.

ii. **A LIBRARY** : For which books would be purchased from the non-recurring and recurring provisions; copies of old journals will be maintained and useful booklets relating to development programmes will be published by concerned agencies.

iii. **A READING ROOM** : With wall papers and newspapers appropriate for adult learners, informative and entertaining journals, developmental literature etc.

iv. **A CHARCHA MANDAL** : (Discussion group): For discussion on common problems and to evolve a strategy to overcome the same based on the opinion of the majority

v. **TRAINING PROGRAMMES:** Simple and of short duration relating to such subjects as health and family welfare, new developments in agriculture and animal husbandry, conservation of energy, improved chulha should be organised etc. JSN may also help the local youth to benefit from various vocational training programmes.

vi. **GAMES AND SPORTS** And other activities to be organised by laying the stress on indigenous sports, walking excursions, cycling trips in groups, etc. if savings are available, visit by bus to development projects, could also be arranged.

vii. **RECREATIONAL AND CULTURAL ACTIVITIES:** Particularly traditional and folk forms of art, rural theatre, puppetry etc should be organised.

viii. **AN INFORMATION WINDOW:** For securing information on various developmental programmes. Information and material suitable for neo-literates has to be procured from the concerned development agencies.

ix. **COMMUNICATION CENTRE:** Where community radio, audio cassette player-cum-recorder may be provided. To begin with, TV and VCR may also be provided in the JSNs of 40 Technology Demonstration Districts (TDDS).

3. CLIENTELE OF THE JANA SHIKSHANA NILAYAM

The functions and objectives of the JSN reveal that it will be able to serve the following categories of persons.

(i) The neo-literates who complete the functional literacy course.

(ii) Those who become literate through the mass programme for functional literacy

(iii) School drop-outs

(iv) Pass-outs of primary schools

(v) Pass-outs of Non-formal Education Programme and

(vi) All other members of the community so far as group activities and cultural programmes are concerned.

The successful implementation of the scheme of JSN largely depends upon the capability and efficiency of the prerak in performing the functions ascribed to him. In view of this, the scheme of JSN has clearly defined the functions of the preraks.

4. FUNCTIONS OF THE PRERAKS

The functions of the preraks were as follows.

(i) To conduct activities of a JSN with the help of volunteers.

(ii) To organise post-literacy and continuing education programmes in the village other than the ones in which the JSN is situated.

(iii) Taking newspapers, journals and books at the time of his visit to those villages, and organising inter-village sports and cultural competitions.

5. PRE-REQUISITE QUALITIES OF PRERAK

In order to performs the above roles effectively, the prerak should be a local person with proven leadership qualities. However the scheme of JSN envisages that a person can be selected as prerak, if he is haying the following qualities.

(i) Has given evidence of interest in serving the community, particularly women and economically deprived sections of the society .

(ii) Has leadership quality and ability to take voluntary help of the local youth.

(iii) Has sufficient free time, atleast 3-4 hours every evening.

(iv) Has atleast Matriculate qualification to be reduced to VIIth class level in case of specially gifts person, women and persons belonging to SC/ST.

The Post-literacy and follow-up programmes envisaged through the JSN is to provide suitable educational environment to retain and to nurture the literacy learned by illiterates to prevent them to relapse into the ocean of illiteracy. Further, JSNs were established to perform, various functions both for the benefit of the participants and as well as community. The prerak, in-charge of JSN plays a crucial role in organising the various activities. Though only 400 JSNs were functioned at the time of data collection, in the Rayalaseema districts but in view of the ongoing total literacy programmes in all the districts of Rayalaseema region more post-literacy and continuing education facilities has to be created to cover the newly made literates.

6. REVIEW OF RELATED LITERATURE

Research studies which focus their attention on different aspects of the functioning of JSNs may through light on the ways and means of organising JSNs effectively. A few research studies conducted by the researchers (Vasumathi, 1992; Nair, Omanna and Rehim, 1992; Muthuchamy, 1992; Adilakshmi 1993; Operations Research Group-DAE, 1994; Reddeppa, 1994; SRC, 1995; Janardhana, 1996; Mohanty and Prusty 1996) have been identified and presented with a view to get better insight into the research problem to be attempted.

Vasumathi (1992) studied the functioning of Scheme of Jana Shikshana Nilayam in Kannur district of Kerala and found that majority of the Jana Shikshana Nilayams were catering to about 100 to 500 beneficiaries. It is also found that majority of the uses of Jana Shikshana Nilayam were neo-literate, mostly belongs to women, all the JSNs were having buildings with sufficient furniture and a separate room for reading and all them were electrified.

With regard to the background of the preraks, it was found that majority of the preraks had upto 5 years of experience as instructors and affiliated to some cultural and sports clubs. The findings with regard to the administration disclosed that all programme officers were men majority of them were not undergone any training in literacy and not satisfied with regard to the facilities provided to them. Further they have not received adequate cooperation from their higherups in organising training programmes, supply of Teaching learning materials, mobilizing resources etc. All the JSNs have organised various cultural and co-curricular activities such as Literacy Jathas, Street Dramas, meetings, awareness campaigns, study tours and family meetings.

The study also identified the problems/difficulties of the preraks such as viz., Lack of adequate funds, Lack of cooperation from the

Governmental departments Lack of interest among the neo-literates, in adequate Neo-literate literature, in adequate physical facilities, lack of play ground for conducting sports meet, lack of adequate public supports, etc.

Nair, Omanna and Rehim (1992) studied the programmes and activities of JSN organised by Nehru Yuvak Kendra in Kerala. The findings reveals that an equal number of men and women were involved as preraks and majority of preraks in the age group of 19-20 years with annual income ranges from 1,000 to 2,000 rupees. On the other hand nearly half of them belongs to backward communities.

The study also discloses that majority of preraks had adequate experience in Total Literacy Campaign as instructors and master trainers, majority of the preraks were affiliated to some cultural or sports organisations, and interest in social work prompted them to join as preraks.

With regard to physical facilities available, one third of the JSNs were possessed improvised teaching aids half of them had a separate reading room none of them are having a own building. The major source for the books and the other material were found to be Nehru Yuvak Kendras and all of them were receiving news papers. The dropouts inadequate training and funds were the major problems of the JSNs.

Muthuchamy (1992) studied the role performance of the preraks and found that there is a discrepancy between the ideal performance and actual performance of preraks in their role as organises of literacy/ post-literacy activities (56.25%) generator of awareness (62.60%) organiser of cultural and recreational programmes (56%) mobilises of resources (60.64%) records of educational activities (35.20%) professional devotion (61.20%) guidance activity (65.86%), supervisory functions (38.88%). In addition to above the study also identified the following problems of the preraks in their role performance, lack of interest among the people for learning, lack of effective planning, inadequate physical facilities and proper place for JSN, Non availability graded materials, lack of sufficient training for the preraks, limited knowledge possessed by the preraks, in adequate supply of Neo-literate materials, lack of motivation on the part of learners, lack of transport facilities, inadequate audio-visual aids, difficulty in bringing the experts to the villages, in ability of the prerak in contacting the specialists, non-availability of the total talents, non-existing of mahila mandals and youth clubs, lack of measuring instruments of functionality and awareness among the adult learners, lack of technical/professional skills, inadequate training, inability in identifying the solution for the slow learners, personal and social problems of the preraks.

Further, the study also revealed that women preraks, preraks with more than 30 years of age, other than S.C.. Preraks, better qualified, more experienced were found to the best role performers.

Adilakshmi (1993) investigated into the working conditions of the JSNs and found that the preraks organising JSNs were confined to the post-literacy activities alone. None of the JSNs were provided with audio-visual facilities. The study also revealed that there is no difference between the working conditions of JSN organised by the preraks with different age and experienced groups.

Reddeppa (1993) identified the determinants of prerak effectiveness. The findings of the study reveals that the working preraks of the JSN were from men, unprevilised sections, poor low educated, less experienced, younger, married and belongs to agricultural background groups. The results shows that women, forward caste, agricultural background, more income, more educated, married elders more positive attitude were found to be the determinants of effective preraks.

Padmanabhaiah and Kumaraswami (1995) identified the problems faced by the monitors in organising Jana Chaityanya Kendras for providing post-literacy and continuing education facilities for the neo-literates.

The state Resources Centre of Karnataka (1995) conducted an observational study to identify the role of JSN in continuing education.

The findings of the study were as follows. (1) Majority of the libraries of JSN were kept open between 8 A.M. to 10 A.M. and 4 P.M. to 6 P.M. and few of them were opened through out the day. (2) Educators visit JSNs to read news papers only. However school going children/school dropouts were the regard users of JSN's. (3) Story books and thrillers were found to be popular. (4) Inadequate availability of the books on professionally related and vocation related or job related literature in

JSN. (5) Majority of the preraks lacked motivation, insight and vision for running JSN and failed to meet the demands of public in terms of needed information/skills and training of the local youth. (6) Although majority of the preraks were well qualified, no evidence of success of JSNs in terms of furthering literacy and continuing education. (7) No evidence and support for the claims of conducting cultural, sports, and other literary activities. (8) A large quantity of good quality reading materials were kept ideal in JSNs. The preraks does not know to bring awareness in public. Both preraks and public were indifferent to the spirit and mission of JSNs. (9) The facilities provided to the preraks namely bicycle, sweeing missions, the radio two-in-one, were missing from JSN or they are miss used by the prerak and the public, sports material, Musical instrument did required chronic replacement of repair. (10) Only 5% of the JSNs were found to be functioned effectively in one aspect or the other. (11) Only 37 JSNs had its own buildings. (12) The post literacy centres, the Grama Shikshana Samithies have become almost in effective/disfunctional as a result the JSNs have become handicapped. (13) The preraks of the JSNs were under paid and thus positions are insecured. There is a great deal of delay and dis organisation in the payment. (14) The payment of contingent grants to all the functioning JSN involved a great amount of practice. (15) There is a great deal of administrative and inter departmental procedures involved in providing electricity to JSNs. (16) The functioning of JSNs in the state where non-existence of own buildings for were struggling for their survival because of the imposed interference of donor institutions or other extraneous factors like theft, lack of place, remoteness etc. (17) The JSNs have been ignored wilfully with regard to their role in TLCs and education for all. JSNs have no place nor responsibility in the net work of any of their movement. As a result they were neither obligated to nor accountable to literacy movements.

Operations Research Group (DAE 1994) has evaluated the functioning of the scheme of JSNs for highlighting its strengths and overcome the existing deficiencies. The major findings of the study were as follows.

1. OVERALL IMPACT

The continuing Education programme, on the whole, has a positive impact on the rural population. The provision of JSN facilities has succeeded in enhancing the demand for education, particularly continuing education, which is apparent from high participation levels. The need for grass-roots level institutions catering to continuing education in being acutely felt in post - TLC districts.

2. PARTICIPATION IN JSN ACTIVITIES

(a) Library - The library is found to be the most popular activity of the JSN and is used by people from all age-groups. There is a strong demand for a more versatile library facility and for adoption of a decentralized process of selection of reading materials. There were more books available to cater to formally educated than the neo-literates.

(b) Sports, recreational and cultural activities-sports was observed to be the second most popular activity of the JSN. Availability of sports equipments and musical instruments had served the purpose of making the JSN more attractive to the rural people. However, in most JSNs condition of sports materials was found to be bad.

(c) Literacy classes - Holding of evening classes is perceived to be an important function of the Preraks by he community and a majority of the Preraks did organise such classes. Largest share of evening class attends were semi-literates from Adult Education Programmes.

(d) Discussion groups - The general level of awareness among the learners groups regarding charcha mandals organised through JSNs was observed 'to be very low'. Charcha Mandals catered mostly to exclusive male groups and there is not much participation by women largely because of the conservative social norms and the dual responsibilities which they have to perform at home and in the field.

(e) Training programmes - Organizing training programmes has been found to be most neglected activity of the JSNs less than 20% of the Preraks reported to have organised any such activity. Also, JSNs were hardly used by other Government departments to impart training or knowledge regarding various schemes or any other developmental issues.

3. CATERING CAPACITY OF JSNS

The norm of having one JSN per 5,000 population was found to be too optimistic. In practice, each JSN caters to less than 250 people. For hilly states like Mizoram, the concept of having one JSN to cover 4-5 villages becomes redundant because of conditions of terrain and refused accessibility which clearly indicates that separate set of norms will have to be evolved for allocating JSNs in different regions.

4. INFRASTRUCTURAL/RESOURCE SUPPORT

(a) No budget has been provided for training of Preraks and in most of the States, the Preraks deployed to run the JSN's have not received any training at all. Selection of the Preraks in many of the States has not been made in accordance with the prescribed criteria. In places where village Education committees were associated in the selection process, the Preraks chosen were found to be more acceptable to the community.

(b) Shortage of manpower and infrastructure available to the District Adult Education Officers (DAEOs) have adversely effected the supervision and monitoring of the programme. No specific budgetary provisions have been made in the programme to cover expenses on supervision and monitoring. After the withdrawal if RELP, no formal posts of Project Officers or Assistant Project Officers exist to provide an organizational structure for the management of the JSNs. This lack of manpower and absence of adequate interaction between the DAEOs and the Preraks have adversely affected the programme performance.

(c) Delays in payment of honorarium to Preraks have effectively reduced the commitment level leading even to closure of JSNs, insufficient amount of honorarium is also perceived to be one of the major reasons for non-performance of Preraks. Crucial out of pocket expenses of the Preraks like organizing training programmes, travelling and postage costs are not reimbursed through the programme, which has further hampered the performance of the JSNs.

(d) In most States, the expectation of donation of a space by the community to run the JSN have not been realized. The current JSN programme does not have a budget provision for reimbursing the amount paid for rented accommodation. Quite often, preraks have been forced to run the JSNs from their own residences which has drastically hindered community participation.

Janardhan Rao (1996) enquired into the problems faced by the monitors in Jana Chaitanya Kendras. In order to bring out the nature of the problems, the problem items were categorised into organisation, administration, environment, co-operative and material related. To study the association between problems and personal characteristics viz., Sex, Caste, Occupation, Income, Experience, Education and Marital status were identified. The finding of the study revealed that lack of suitable materials, place for JSK, co-operation experts, village leaders, motivation among the neo-literates were found to be the prominent problems. In addition availability of young, and in-experienced monitors, involvement caste, religion and village politics and fraction were also found to be prominent problems in organising JCKs.

Mohanty and Prusty (1996) identified the problems of functioning of JSNs in Orissa and the finding of the study were as follows.

i. Majority of the JSNs were situated near to the home of sarpanch or chairman and not suitable to the learners.

ii. Half of the JSNs lacked fundamental infrastructure and learners faced trouble in reading at centres in summer and rainy seasons.

iii. No library and TV or Radio facilities were provided to any JSN.

iv. JSNs were not received the Teaching materials adequately and in due-time. Even the quality of the supplied things new of low level, whereas cost was high.

v. Though charcha mandals were working in many JSNs local people were not benefitted by it as they did not give due importance to local needs, occupations, professions having practical or income orientation future.

vi. Instructions for women on their daily life were negligible.

vii. File and record-based supervision was also fully with corruptions and malpractices and as a result money and materials of JSN of a developing nation were getting misused.

viii. Majority of preraks were regular and were highly educated. Though some exceptionally highly educated preraks tried to act democratically, their hands were tightened by higher authorities. Some also suffered from financial crisis and lack of conscious support from local people to activate JSNs.

ix. More or less, the cultural activities like Ganesh Puja, Saraswathi Puja, Independence day were observed, by neglecting the important days like World Literacy Day, World Health Day, Environment Day, Netaji Jayanthi etc. which were not known to rural illiterates and neo-literates and not known to rural illiterates and which could inculcate different values among them.

x. Lack of trained missionary-Zeal-bearer-Instructors kept interested learners aloof of the JSN.

From the above review, it is clear that not many studies were conducted on the functioning of the JSNs. The available studies were of peripheral and were not able to throw much of the light on the activities undertaken inside and outside the JSNs.

The knowledge in the functioning of JSNs in terms of various activities undertaken inside and outside the JSN and in the community will be more helpful in formulating suitable strategies for providing better services and to rectify the defects if any, in the implementation of the scheme.

If the JSNs were not able to perform the functions for which they were created, then the entire effect made in literating the illiterates will go a waste. Hence, the knowledge of the activities that were undertaken inside the JSN and in the community will go a long way in formulating suitable strategies in effective implementation of the scheme of JSN. As the review of literature has not disclosed much in this direction, the present study was formulated to investigate the functioning of the JSNs in Rayalaseema region of Andhra Pradesh.

2

STATEMENT OF THE PROBLEM

The chapter states the problem of the study, scope of the study, need of the study, objectives of the study, Hypothesis, variables incorporated in the study and limitations of the study.

1. STATEMENT OF THE STUDY

The intention of the study is "To study the functioning of the JSNs in Rayalaseema region of A.P.".

2. SCOPE OF THE STUDY

As the aim of the investigation is to study the functioning of the JSNs, hence it is proposed to measure the effectiveness of the JSNs in terms of the performance of the various functions. Further it is also aimed to study the influence of the factors viz. availability of infrastructure, community support and the community attitude towards functioning of JSNs, availability of reading materials and reading interests of the neo-literates. In addition it is also aims at measuring the preraks attitude, toward various activities of the JSN the problems of the preraks and to study the factors influencing the JSN effectiveness.

3. NEED OF THE STUDY

With a view to preventing the relapse of neo-literates into illiteracy and ensuring that the basic literacy skills acquired by them are reinforced, retained and applied in day-to-day life situations, National Literacy Mission envisaged institutionalization of post-literacy and continuing education arrangements through setting-up of Jana Shikshana Nilayams throughout the country. The basic objective in the planning of the scheme of Jana Shikshana Nilayams is to ensure remediation, continuation of learning activities through facilities of reading room and Library in JSNs and also application of literacy skills for improvement in their actual living conditions. The important functions of a JSN include conduct of evening classes for 3-4 hours once in a week for up-gradation of literacy and numeracy skills, provide library facilities with a provision of books on developmental programmes and other subjects useful in day to day life, provision of reading room with provisions of wall posters and news papers appropriate for adult learners, informative journals, developmental literatures etc. Organisation of short duration training programmes, conduct of charcha mandals, sports and other adventurous activities and also, serves as a window and issues of national concern. The prerak, incharge of JSN plays a crucial role in organising the various activities.

The selection of Chittoor district for implementation of total literacy campaign, and as a result of intensive drive for eradication of illiteracy resulting in creation of large pool of new-literates, there is a need for expansion of post-literacy and continuing education facilities. In view of the expansion of the programmes, there is every need to evaluate the on-going programme to identify the strengths and weaknesses for replication and rectification.

The utility of the library depends on the quality and relevance of the reading materials available in the JSN, the reading materials approved by the Government of A.P. are being supplied to all the JSNs irrespective of local needs and demands. Further for successful organisation of the various activities of JSNs and in creation of proper educational environment requires peoples participation and community support. Elicitation of peoples participation and community support largely depends on the preraks efficiency, leadership and capacity in identifying and overcoming the problems that they encountered in the implementation of various activities of JSN. The effectiveness of the prerak also depends on the attitude of the prerak, infrastructure available, the quality of the training received and the degree of community support received etc. Hence, in view of the above, the present study was formulated to investigate into the functioning of JSNs in Rayalaseema region with an aim to identify the factors responsible for its success or otherwise to guide the future programme lest the money, materials and manpower invested in this programme as well as on the adult education programme is going to be a waste. Further, in order to maintain the quality of the programme, it is necessary to have a suitable guidelines for proper mode of selection and training of post-literacy workers, selection of reading materials, and suitable strategies for creation of conducive environment. In view of the above the present study was formulated in this direction with the following objectives.

4. OBJECTIVES

The objectives of the study are

i. To measure the effectiveness of JSN based on its performance of various activities.

ii. To find out the availability of infrastructure for the organisation of JSNs.

iii. To ascertain the community attitude towards the functioning of JSNs.

iv. To identify the reading interests of the community and to compare with the reading materials available with the JSNs.

v. To prepare a profile of an effective prerak.

vi. To measure the attitude of preraks towards the various aspects of JSNs.

vii. To identify the problems faced by the preraks in organising the JSNs.

viii. To assess the community support received for the effective functioning of the JSNs.

5. HYPOTHESES

In view of the above objectives, the following hypothesis were formulated for testing.

i. The availability of the proper infrastructure is likely to enhance the functioning of the JSNs.

ii. Positive attitude of the community towards the JSN is closely related with its effective functioning.

iii. The effective functioning of the JSNs depends on the availability of the suitable reading materials.

iv. Positive attitude of preraks towards various aspects of JSN leads to the effective functioning of JSNs.

v. Lesser the problems faced by the preraks in organising the JSNs higher will be the effective functioning of JSN.

vi. The effective functioning of the JSN depends on the degree of the support received from the community.

6. VARIABLES STUDIED

The aim of the study is to find out the functioning of the JSNs. The functioning of the JSNs depends on its performance of various roles and hence the effectiveness of the JSN depends on various factors. In view of the various factors involved in the effective performance of the JSNs, the following variables were chosen to study the association with the effective functioning of the JSN and differences if any among the different variables in their influence on functioning of the JSNs.

7. DEPENDENT VARIABLE

The effective functioning of the JSNs in terms of the performance of its roles was chosen as the dependent variables of the study.

8. INDEPENDENT VARIABLES

The factors viz., community attitude, prerak attitude, problems of the prerak, job-performance of infrastructure and community support were selected as independent variables.

9. LIMITATIONS OF THE STUDY

i. The study is limited to 100 JSNs functioning in Rayalaseema region of Andhra Pradesh.

ii. Only a few factors were chosen as independent variables to study their influence on the functioning of JSNs.

iii. Only the preraks were chosen as representatives of the programme functionaries.

The method adopted in the study, the method of construction of the research tools, data collection, statistical techniques employed were presented in the Chapter III.

3

METHOD OF INVESTIGATION

The present chapter describes the method adopted for the development of tools, pilot study, locale, sample of the study, administration of the tool, collection of data, analysis of data etc.

To test the hypotheses framed for the study requires certain tools to measure the selected variables, viz., community attitude, prerak attitude, reading interests problem of the prerak, job performance of the preraks communities support and JSN efficiency. Apart from the above a list of the items of infrastructure available, community support received, personal information of the preraks was also to be collected.

DEVELOPMENT OF RESEARCH TOOLS

Community Attitude Scale

In order to measure the attitude of the community towards various activities of JSN, a measure is required. From the review of the literature (Chapter -II) it is clear that there are no suitable tools readily available for measuring the attitude of the community towards JSN. Hence the investigator had to develop an attitude scale for the purpose of the present study. Out of the available options for developing attitude scale, it was decided to develop the attitude scale in the lines suggested by the Likert in view of its advantages. [Shukla, 1972, Adams (1964)].

a. Preparation of Preliminary Form

As a first step in preparation of attitude scale, the field functionaries, community, village level literacy committee members were interviewed and generated a list of items depecting the attitude statements. In addition to the above, relevant literature was reviewed, relevant items were pooled and supplemented to the list. The list of descriptive items thus obtained were subjected to scrutiny and relevant statements were added to the list. After this all the statements together were reviewed and rewritten to avoid ambiguity and overlapping.

The preliminary form thus prepared consisted of 40 statements of which 20 items were supposed to represent positive attitude and the remaining 20 items were supposed to represent negative attitude. This was presented to a panel of 5 experts in the field of adult education with a request to suggest omissions and modifications where ever necessary. The suggestions of the experts were carried out. At this stage there were 30 items in the preliminary form.

b. Rating Procedure for the Items

Before subjecting the tool for conducting the pilot study, the rating procedure was also to be determined. In doing so, the various types of rating methods viz numerical rating, cumulated points rating, multiple choice method etc, were carefully examined. Keeping in view the level of the proposed sample subjects of the study and the opinion of the majority experts in the field it was felt that the rating should be as simple as possible to avoid unnecessary mental strain and confusion among the subjects while giving the response.

In the light of the above, the popular numerical rating scale consisting of five descriptive cues was chosen. The five descriptive cues viz strongly agree, agree, undecided, disagree, strongly disagree were found to be more appropriate for rating the items chosen for the community attitude scale. The respondents were supposed to agree with any one of the alternative cues, to mark the level of attitude possessed by the community towards the various activities of the JSN.

c. Pilot Study

The purpose of present study is to develop an attitude scale to measure community attitude towards JSN activities. Hence, the appropriate sample for pilot study was the community people. For the purpose of the present Pilot Study a sample of 100 villagers was selected at random from different JSNs in Chittoor district of Andhra Pradesh. Care was also taken to see that the sample of villagers chosen represented different socio-economic status and different age groups.

The items in the attitude scale were read out to the villagers and the response given by them were noted down by the investigator accordingly.

d. Scoring of the Items

The items were scored in according with the common practice of assigning numerical values to the five categories of responses. The numerical values assigned to the ratings of positive and negative statements as shown below.

TABLE 1 : SCORING OF THE STATEMENTS

S.No	Nature of response	Numerical values assigned	
		Positive items	Negative items
1.	Strongly agree	5	1
2.	Agree	4	2
3.	Undecided	3	3
4.	Disagree	2	4
5.	Strongly disagree	1	5

e. Selection of the Items

In order to determine the discriminative power and usefulness of statements chosen for the scale, the 't' value for each of the items was calculated as per the procedure suggested by Edwards 1969. Items that had calculated `t' value equal to or grater than 1.75 were selected for inclusion in the final form and all other items with `t' values less than 1.75 were discarded. Based on this procedure 10 items were discorded. Thus out of 30 items chosen for preliminary form 20 items were selected in the final form. Cf this 10 items were positive indicators and 10 negative indicators.

f. Reliability of the Scale

For the purpose of the present scale test Retest reliability was adopted to examine the reliability of the scale. This was done by obtaining the ratings for the scale with an interval of two weeks between the first and second administration of the scale to the same set of 100 villagers. The correlation coefficient between the two administrations was 0.89 and was significant at 0.01 level. Hence the attitude scale was considered to be highly reliable.

g. Validity of the Scale

The present attitude scale developed on the lines described above possessed satisfactory validity with reference to the content, Items and Intrinsic validity. The description of details relating to the validity of the scale was as follows.

Content Validity

Content validity indicates how adequately is the content of a test-sampling the domain about which inferences are to be made. Further, when taken collectively the items should constitute representative sample of the variable that is measured. The present attitude scale was developed keeping the above in view. As already described, items for the scale were collected from different sources viz. Neo-literates, Instructors. Supervisors and preraks. Further, they were also supplemented by a review of related literature and also by interviewing selected programme functionaries and experts to make sure that all possible items were included. Thus it can be reasonable assumed that the instrument possesses satisfactory content validity.

Item Validity

Item validity stresses the extent to which the item predicts segregation of sample into those with high versus those with low criterion scores. The discriminative power of each of the present scale was established by calculating their 't' values. Thus the items chosen for both parts of the scale were found to be effectively valid.

Intrinsic Validity

Intrinsic validity indicates the degree to which a test measures what it purport to measure. This can also be stated as how well the obtained scores measures the tests true score component. Square root of the reliability value of the scale means its intrinsic validity. Thus the intrinsic validity of the attitude scale was $\sqrt{0.92 - 0.96}$ which can be assumed that the score has highly satisfying intrinsic validity.

Prerak Attitude Scale

An attitude scale to measure the attitude of preraks towards various aspects of JSN was necessary for the purpose of present study. The review of literature discloses that no suitable tool is readily available for measuring the attitude of preraks. Hence the investigator has to develop an attitude scale to suite the purpose of the present study. For developing the present scale Likert technique was adopted. In developing the present scale also all the steps followed in developing community attitude scale described in the previous pages was also followed. However, a brief description of the development of the scale is as follows.

The preliminary form of the attitude scale was developed by pooling all the relevant items from different sources viz, field functionaries of Adult Education, Programme participants, community and experts in the field. The items thus generated constitutes both positive and negative indicators of Adult Education. The list thus prepared was submitted to a panel of 5 experts with a request to suggest omissions and modifications where ever necessary. The rating procedure as described earlier was followed, i.e. the rating procedure with 5 descriptive cues of strongly agree, Agree, Un-decided, Disagree and strongly disagree were fitted to the scale with numerical values of 5,4,3,2, and 1 respectively.

The preliminary attitude scale at this stage consisted of 26 items out of which 13 represents unfavourable items and 13 favourable items. The preliminary form was subjected to a pilot study on preraks chosen at random. The procedure suggested by Edwards (1969) was followed for identifying the discriminative power and usefulness of the items. As a result of the adopting of this procedure 9 items were discarded and 17 items were retained in the final form.

a. Reliability and Validity

In order to establish the reliability of the scale test retest method was adopted by adminstring the scale to a same set of 50 preraks with an interval of two weeks. The calculated 'r' value between the two ratings is 0.92 which is significant at 0.01 level.

The validity of the scale was also established through content, items and intrinsic validity. The scale was found to be highly valid in terms of the above.

READING INTEREST RATING SCALE

The reading interests of the neo-literates can be identified by using a number of ways. Interests can be identified through the books that the people would read, views expressed in a group discussion, by asking the persons directly etc. The review of literature reveals that different techniques has been utilised for identifying the reading interests viz. Interview method observation techniques, rating scales, check list etc. However for the purpose of the present study the rating technique was utilised for not only identifying the reading interest but also the intensity of the items chosen. Further the rating technique has a number of advantages like it takes less time, minimum training is required, the range of its application is very wide etc.

Development of the Tool

On the basis of the information gathered through the discussions with neo-literates, Preraks, instructors project administrators, a list of possible reading interests were prepared. This list was supplemented with additional reading interest items gathered from review of literature. At this stage the list has 120 reading interest items.

The list of the items thus prepared was submitted to a panel of 5 experts with a request to go through them and suggest for inclusion and omission of items. The suggestions of the experts were carried out by re-drafting the list of the reading interest.

The aim of the study is to identify the reading interests along with the intensity of the desire for reading the item. Keeping in view of the background of the sample and the aim of the study, it was decided to have a 5 point numerical scale with descriptive cues viz. Strongly agree, Agree, undecided, Disagree and Strongly disagree with numerical values of 5,4,3,2 and 1 was assigned to the above descriptive cues for measuring the intensity of the interest. The respondents were suppose to agree with any one of the alternative cues to indicate the intensity of their reading interest.

The preliminary form of reading interest rating scale thus prepared consisted of two sections. Section one deals with the personal information of the sample and section two consisted of 160 reading interest items.

Pilot Study

The preliminary form of reading interest scale was subjected to a pilot study. As the aim of the study is to identify the reading interests of neo-literates, the appropriate sample for pilot study, was the neo-literates. For conducting the pilot study a sample of 100 neo-literates were selected at random from different JSNs. Care was also taken to see that the sample represented different socio-economic status. The items in the rating scale was read out the neo-literates and responses were noted down by the investigator accordingly.

The statements were score in accordance with the common practice of assigning the numerical value to the 5 categories of responses. The numerical values of 5,4,3,2 and 1 were accorded to the descriptive cues viz strongly agree, Agree, Undecided, Disagree and Strongly disagree respectively.

Selection of the Items

In order to find out the usefulness and discriminative power of the items the schedules were arranged in descending order based on the obtained interest scores by the neo-literates. Top 27 and bottom 27 schedules were chosen for calculating the 't' values for all the items. Based on the procedure suggested by Edward (1969) all the items with 't' values of 1.75 and above were selected and those items with less than 1.75 't' values were rejected. Thus out of 160 items chosen for preliminary form 147 items were selected for the final form.

Reliability and Validity of the Scale

For the purpose of present study test retest reliability method was adopted to examine the reliability of the scale. The scale was administered to a selected sample of 50 neo-literates twice with an interval of two weeks. The correlation co-efficient between the two ratings was 0.92 which is significant at 0.01 level. Therefore the reading interest rating scale was considered as having high reliability.

The validity of the scale was also established in the form of content validity, item validity and intrinsic validity and found to be highly valid

JOB PERFORMANCE OF THE PRERAK

For the purpose of the study, a measure that can rate the performance of the prerak with reference to be roles assigned to him, was necessary. From the review of literature it appears that no systematic attempt has been made by any investigation in the field at Adult Education to develop and standardized the test that could rate Adult Education preraks. Thus in absence of any standard instrument to measure job performance of the preraks, necessitated to develop a rating scale to rate the job performance of the preraks. In developing the rating scale, the following steps were followed.

a. Preparation of the Preliminary Form

First a list of items that were supposed to describe the term job performance of the prerak from different angles were pool together from different sources like preraks, participants of the programme, Administrators of the programme, experts in the field etc. Further the list thus prepared was supplemented with a list of items drawn from review of literature and the guidelines issued by Government of India prescribing the scheme of JSNs and roles to be performed by the preraks. The list thus prepared was submitted to a panel of 5 experts with a request to scrutiny the statements for their appropriateness and for refinement. The opinion of the experts were carried. At this stage there are 58 items in the preliminary form of Prerak role performance rating scale.

b. Rating Procedure of the Items

For the purpose of present study, numerical rating technique was chosen keeping in view of its advantages, background of the sample and the opinion of the experts. In rating the items, the popular numerical rating scale consisting of 5 descriptive cues were chosen. The five descriptive cues strongly agree, Agree, Undecided, Disagree, strongly disagree were found to be more appropriate for rating the job performance items chosen. The respondents were supposed to agree with any one of the alternative cues to mark the level of performance of the prerak in that particular role under consideration.

c. Pilot Study

The best judges to deal about the level of performance of the preraks were the neo-literates and the community people, as these two groups of the people were influenced by him through his various activities. A sample of neo-literates and community 50 each (100) was chosen at random as sample for the pilot study. The preliminary form of prerak job performance rating scale was administered to them. The items in the rating scale were read out to the sample and the response given by the sample were noted down by the investigator accordingly.

d. Scoring of the Items

The scoring of the items was done in accordance with the general practice of assigning numerical values to the five categories of responses chosen as follows.

TABLE 2: SCORING OF THE ITEMS

S.No.	Nature of response	Numerical value assigned
1.	Strongly agree	5
2.	Agree	4
3.	Undecided	3
4.	Disagree	2
5.	Strongly disagree	1

Selection of Items

To find out the discriminative power and usefulness of the items chosen for prerak job performance scale the 't' values for each of the items in the scale were calculated as per the procedure suggested by Edward (1969). Items that had calculated 't' value equal to, and greater than 1.75 were selected for inclusion in the final form and those with 't' values less than 1.75 were discorded. Based on this procedure 11 items were discorded. Thus out of 57 items chosen for the preliminary scale 46 items were selected to retain in the final form.

f. Reliability of the Scale

The scale developed for measuring a particular Characteristics of individual representing specific category will be sound only when its reliability is established. For this purpose test-retest reliability of the scale developed was examined. This was done by obtaining the rating for the scale twice with an interval of three weeks between the First and Second administration of the instrument to the same set of (50 each) neo-literates and community representatives. The correlation and coefficient between the rating was 0.84 which is significant at 0.01 level. Therefore the rating scale may be considered as having high reliability.

g. Validity of the Scale

Any instrument developed for measuring a particular aspect will be considered appropriate only when its validity is proved. The prerak job performance scale developed on the lines described above possess satisfactory validity with reference to the content items and intrinsic validity. The description of details relating to validity of the scale as follows.

Content Validity

Content validity means establishment and evaluation of the relevance of the test items individually and as a whole. Every item should be a sampling of that aspect which the test purports to measure. Further when taken collectively, the items consistitute a representative sample of the variable that is measured. The present scale was developed keeping the above in view. As already described, items for the scale were collected from different sources viz. Monitors, Preraks, Learners, Neo-literates and community. Further they were also supplemented by a review of related literature and also by interviewing selected instructors/experts to make sure that all possible items were included thus it can be reasonable assume that the instrument possess satisfactory content validity.

Item Validity

Item validity stresses the number of discriminations of the desired sort that the item is capable of making. It emphasis the extent to which the item predicts segregation of examines into those with high versus those with low criterion scores. The discriminative power of each of the items of the present scale was established by calculating the 't' values as described above. Thus the items chosen for the scale were found to be effectively valid.

Intrinsic Validity

Intrinsic validity indicates the degree to which a test measures what it purports to measure. Thus it can also be stated as how well the obtained scores measures the tests true score component. Square root of the reliability value of the scale means its intrinsic validity. Thus the intrinsic validity of the scale was $\sqrt{0.84}$ -0.916 which can be assumed as highly satisfying intrinsic validity score.

h. Brief Description of the Final Form of Prerak Job Performance

The final form of prerak job performance scale developed in the lines described above consisted of two sections Section - A relates to the back ground of the preraks and Section - B of the scale consists of job performance items. Each item can be rated on any of the five response categories viz. Strongly agree, Agree, undecided, Disagree and Strongly disagree which carries numerical values 5,4,3,2 and 1 respectively. In view of this the score of the scale will range between 46 and 230 points. The full format of the scale is as shown in the appendix.

PRERAK PROBLEM INVENTORY

One of the aim of the study is to identify the problems of the preraks in performing their job. Keeping this in view the available literature was review and found that not much efforts has been made in developing a suitable and comprehensive scale for measuring the problems of the preraks. Hence an attempt was made by the investigator to develop a prerak problem inventory on scientific lines not only to identify the problems but also the intensity of the problem checked by the preraks.

a. Development of the Preliminary Form

In order to develop the inventory a large number of possible problem items were pooled together from difference sources like preraks, community, programme administrator, participants of the programme, experts in the field etc. The list was also supplemented with a list of items drawn from the review of the literature. The list thus prepared was presented to a panel of 5 experts with a request to suggest to review, revise, modify and delete the items wherever necessary. The suggestions of the experts were carried out and re-drafted the list of the problems. The list thus prepared consisted of 25 problem items.

b. Rating Procedure

As the aim of the study is not only to identify the problems but also to measure the intensity of the problem, hence the appropriate method for this should be a numerical rating scale with simple descriptive cues for rating the items by the sample with easy and accuracy. Hence a five point numerical rating scale consisting of 5 descriptive cues viz. Fully agree, Agree, Undecided, Disagree and Fully disagree having the scores 5,4,3,2 and 1 respectively. The respondents were suppose to agree with any of the alternative cues to indicate the intensity of the problems that they were exposed in discharging their roles.

c. Pilot Study

The purpose of the inventory is to identify the problems of the preraks. Hence the appropriate sample for the pilot study were the preraks. A sample of 100 preraks were selected at random from different JSNs of Rayalaseema region of A.P. Before administering the inventory, care was also taken to see that sample selected should represent the cross section of the society. They were also explained the mode of filling the scale for gathering the accurate data.

d. Selection of Items

Based on the obtained problem scores, the prerak problem inventory response sheets were arranged in descending order. The top 27 and bottom 27 response sheets were chosen to find out the discriminative power and usefulness of the items. The 't' values for each of the items of the two categories of response sheets were calculated and all these items with 't' values of 1.75 and above were retained for the final form and rest of the items with less than the 't' value of 1.75 were discorded as suggested by Edward (1969). Based on the above procedure 8 items were discorded and the final form of inventory consisted of 17 problems.

e. Reliability and Validity of the Tool

The reliability of the tool was established by test retest method. The 'r' value between the two ratings were found to be significant (0.92) at 0.01 level. Further the validity of the inventory was also established in the form of content validity, item validity and intrinsic validity.

In view of the above the prerak problem inventory were found to be highly reliable and valid.

f. Brief Description of the Prerak Problems Inventory

The final form of the prerak problem inventory developed in the lines described above consisted of 17 items. Each ite can be rated on any of the 5 response category namely strongly agree, agree, undecided, disagree and strongly disagree which carried numerical values 5,4,3,2 and 1 respectively. The score on the inventory will range between 17 and 85 points. The full formate of the inventory was presented in the appendix.

VI. JANA SHIKSHANA NILAYAM COMMUNITY SUPPORT SCALE

The pre-requisite for successful organisation of any development programme is the participation and support of the community. This is also so in case of post-literacy programmes. As the scheme of Jana Chaitanya Kendra was conceived not only to organise programmes leading to retention of literary among the target, but also to empower the entire community. No doubt the scheme of JSN has provided certain facilities and amenities to establish itself fermily at the community but in order to accelerate its activities, community support is also essential. In order to identify the extent of the support provided by the community for organisation of the JSN's at the community level, a community support scale was developed.

(a) Preliminary Form

As the intention of the scale is to identify the community support, all the items relating to the community support was collected from different sources like, Monitors, coordinators, Programme administators and from the community. The list thus prepared was supplemented with the items drawn from the review of literature. The list of the items was subjected to scrutiny and relevant statements were added and ambiguous and overlapping items were removed. The preliminary form thus prepared was presented to a panel of 5 experts in the field of adult education with a request to suggest omissions and modifications were ever necessary. The suggestions of the experts where carried out. At this stage there were 25 items in the preliminary form. In order to measure the community support, it was decided to choose the five point numerical rating scale with descriptive ques for measuring the community support.

Pilot Study

One of the objectives of the study is to develop the community support scale and to measure the community support towards various activities of JSN. Hence the appropriate sample for the pilot study was the community itself. For the purpose of the present pilot study, a sample of 100 villagers was selected at random from different JSNs of Chittoor District and the scale was administered to them. The responses were noted down accordingly by the investigator.

Scoring of the Items

The items were scored in accordance with the common practice of assigning numerical values to the five categories of responses. The numerical values assigned to the descriptive ques viz., strongly supported (5), supported (4) neutral (3) not supported (2), and not at all supported (1).

Selection of Items

To find out the discriminative power and usefulness of the items chosen for community support scale, the 't' values for each of the items in the scale were calculated as per the procedure suggested by Edward (1969). As per this procedure items were discorded. Thus out of 25 items chosen for the preliminary scale 17 items were selected to retain in the fonal form

Reliability and Validity of the Scale

The reliability and validity of the scale was established. The reliability of the scale was established by test - retest method. The 'r' value between two ratings were found to be significant (0.94) at 0.01 level. Further the validity of the inventory was also established in the form of content validity, item validity and intrinsic validity. In view of the above, the community support scale was found to be highly reliable and valid.

PERFORMANCE OF JANA SHIKSHANA KENDRAS

The aim of the scheme of Jana Shikshana Kendras is to institutionalise the Post-literacy and continuing education and to ensure retention of literacy skills, provision of facilities to enable the adult learners to continue their learning beyond elementary literacy, and to create scope for application of their learning for improvement of their living conditions. In order to achieve the above, the JSNs has to perform specific functions viz., Organisation of evening classes, maintaining the Library with a reading room, conducting Training Programmes of short duration, organising charcha mandal, conducting sports and games, recreational and cultural activities, and act as a information window and communication centre. The efficiency of the JSN lies in its performance on various roles. In order to identify the performance of the JSNs an enquiry was made to assess the performance of various roles of JSN individually and as a total.

a. Construction of JSN Performance Scale

The performance of JSN as a whole can be identified, by collecting information on the organisation of various activities under different roles. As a first step in the construction of a questionnaire, information on different activities that can be organised by a JSN was collected from the preraks, other programme functionaries, Field trainers, community and prepared a list of activities. The list was supplemented by review of literature and the guidelines issued by the Govt. of India with regard to the functioning of the JSNs. The Questionnaire thus prepared consisted of questions with one word answers, fill-up the blanks, multiple choice items etc. On the whole the questionnaire is an unstructured fact finding one. The questionnaire thus prepared was submitted to a panel of 5 experts with a request to scrutinise, suggest for modifications, additions and designs etc. Further they were also requested to classify the items under different headings. The suggestions of the experts were carried out and redrafted the questionnaire.

The questionnaire thus prepared was administered to a group of 50 preraks chosen randomly to know whether the items were easily understood by the preraks and whether the items possessed the clarity or not. Based on the results obtained and experience gained, the panel of experts were consulted again and redrafted the entire questionnaire.

The items included and nature of information on each of the function of JSN were of follows.

1. Organisation of Evening Classes for Up-gradation of Literacy and Numeracy Skills

In order to identify the JSN activities in organising various activities relating to the up-gradation of literacy numeracy skills, information on timings of the literacy activities, duration, category of adults attending the programme were collected.

2. Library and Reading Room

One of the main functions of the JSN is to maintain a library with a reading room facility. In order to measure the performance of JSN in terms of its role of maintaining library and reading room for retention of literacy and dissemination of information relating to developmental programmes, the information on facilities available in library, visiting hours of the library, who will be visiting the library, frequent visitors, facilities available for preserving the books, conveniences for distribution of books, extent of utility of books, villagers co-operation, rate of return of the books. News papers and Magazines supplied etc. were collected. The information thus generated was pooled to segregate the JSNs based on the performance.

3. Charcha Mandal Activities

The role of Charcha Mandal in JSN is to discuss the common problems of the community and to take suitable measure to overcome the same. In order to study the functioning of the JSNs in terms of the role of charcha mandals, the information on charcha mandal activities were collected on the following aspects viz Frequency of organisation of Charcha Mandals, Aspects discussed in Charcha Mandals, Facilities created for organisation of Charcha Mandals, Decisions taken for solving the community problems, extent of the implementation of decisions, organisation of special charcha Mandal for discussion on women problems, community participation and co-operation in implementation of decisions etc.

4. Organisation of Simple and Short Duration Training Programmes

The JSNs were expected to organise simple and short duration training programmes for creation of awareness in health and family welfare, new developments in agriculture, animal husbandry, conservation of energy etc. Further JSNs were also expected to organise vocational training programmes for the benefit of the youth. In order to identify the JSNs performance in this aspect, information were generated to know whether such programme were organised or not, if yes on what aspects, availability of experts in the village, their background and co-operation, Source of availability of information on developmental programmes, Extent utility of the above information by the community etc.

5. Organisation of Sports and Adventure Activities

Under this JSN were suppose to promote the indigenous sports, walking excursionis, cycling trips in groups, visit to developmental projects etc. In order to assess the JSNs performance in this area, information on type of sports organised, facilities available for organisation of games and sports, sports and games material available, extent of usefulness of the material, women's participation in sports and people visit to developmental agencies etc were collected.

6. Recreational and Cultural Activities

JSN as part of its activities, it is expected to organise traditional and folk forms of art, rural theatre, puppetry etc. In order to identify the performance of the JSN in this area only the information on whether JSN were organised any activity if yes what are they were collected.

7. JENS as a Communication Centre

In order to popularise the JSN activities, the JSNs were expected to utilise the T.V., Radio, Audio casette player etc, if available in the Panchayath for the promotion of JSN activities and to create awareness among the people about the current developments etc. Hence, the information relating to the availability of AV aids was collected.

b. Scoring of the Items

In order to measure the performance of the various roles and JSN as a whole. All the information collected were quantified by assigning numerical values. The values assigned to each item and other aspects were presented in the appendix.

THE LOCALE AND SAMPLE OF THE STUDY

In order to study the functioning of the Scheme of Jana Shikshana Nilayams, Rayalaseema region of Andhra Pradesh was chosen as area of the study. The Rayalaseema region of A.P. consists of 4 districts viz, Anantapur, Chittoor, Cuddapah and Kurnool. The Scheme of Jana Shikshana Nilayams were in operation in all the districts at the time of study. There were about 400 JSNs functioning in all the districts under the control of Government and Non-Governmental agencies. For the purpose of the present study, 100 JSNs were selected randomly for choosing the sample of the study. In the first stage of sample selection, all the preraks working in these JSNs were selected as sample of the study. In the second stage five neo-literates and five community representatives were selected at random from the villages representing the sample JSNs.

THE SAMPLE FRAME OF THE STUDY WERE AS FOLLOW

Preraks
(100)

Neo-literates	Community
(5x100)	(5x100)

Collection of Data

The questionnaire relating to the functioning of the JSNs, Prerak attitude scale, Prerak problem inventory were administered to the preraks individual by the investigator at the time of his visit to the JSNs. The prerak effectiveness scale were administered to the selected sample of community and neo-literates. The reading interest inventory was administered to the neo-literates. The community attitude scale and community support scale was administered to the selected community. In addition to the above the investigator collected the titles of the neo-literate literature supplied to JSNs from the JSN records.

ANALYSIS OF THE DATA

The data thus collected by using different tools were pooled together and subjected to the analysis by using appropriate statistical techniques such as mean, SD, X^2, t-test and Anova.

4

FINDINGS AND DISCUSSION

The scheme of JSN were conceived to create conducive environment for the survival and revival of the literacy by providing yet an another opportunity for the left overs and backward adults to continue their lust for learning. To be specific the objectives of the JSN as envisaged by the scheme were: Provision of facilities for retention, continuing education and application of functional literacy, Dissemination of information, creation of awareness about national concerns, improvement of economic condition, improved productivity, recreation and healthy living etc. The objectives of the scheme reveals that it was conceived to bring a radical change in the socio-economics of the country. In view of its importance, the present study was formulated to study the functioning of the JSNs at the grass-root level and to identify its strengths and weaknesses for replication and for strengthening.

As described earlier the required information was generated from the selected categories of the sample and the data was analysed. The findings of the study was presented in five sections. The Section I describes the working conditions of JSNs interms of location, timings duration and infrastructure available for the JSNs etc. Section II of the chapter describes the performance of various activities of the JSN i.e Library, Organisation of Charcha Mandals, Training and extension programmes, games & sports etc. Section III of the chapters describes the profile of the working preraks interms of their personnel characteristics, their attitude, problems and their effectiveness etc. Chapter IV discloses the reading interests of the neo-literates and the relevance of the available materials to the interest of neo-literates and the last section (Section V) describes the effectiveness of the JSN as a whole and the factors influencing the same.

SECTION - I

JANA SHIKSHANA NILAYAM: LOCATION, TIMINGS, DURATION PHYSICAL AND INFRASTRUCTURE AVAILABLE

The scheme of Jana Shikshana Nilayam was created to ensure Remediation. Continuation of learning activity through libraries with facilities of separate reading room, application of literacy skills for improvement in the actual living conditions. In order to perform the above it is essential to have some basic infrastructure as well as acceptable working conditions for the target group so as to ensure their active participation in all its activities.

Each Jana Shikshana Nilayam is expected to cover about 5,000 persons spread over in a cluster of 4-5 contiguous villages. Hence initially it was suggested to establish JSN on a priority basis in a village where people come forward to support it by providing a suitable accommodation and other overall resources. Further it will be housed in a school building, panchayat building, or any other public building and villagers would be encouraged to put-un an inexpensive hall or accommodating about 50 persons. Further a JSN should organise an evening class for upgradation of literacy and numeracy skills to be organised for 3-4 hours a week. The learners would have the option to come for an hour or also at the time of their convenience on that day. There was an allocation of Rs. 2000/- towards the purchase of equipment (almirah, Petromax, ground table for putting news papers, roller boards etc) and for the purpose of Bicycle (Rs.700). As the above were suggested guide lines for establishing the JSNs and keeping in view of the aim of present investigation, the information on location of JSN, Timings and duration of various activities, Lighting facilities and furniture available with JSNs were collected and presented in the following pages.

i. Location of Jana Shikshana Kendras

The enquiry with regard to the location of the Jana Shikshana Nilayam, Table-1 revealed that the Jana Shikshana Nilayam's were located at Panchayat Offices (42%). Prerak houses (35%) and rest of them in temples (9%), schools (7%) and learners houses (7%). The above findings reveals that the Jana Shikshana Nilayam's were not having proper and permanent housing facilities. It appears that Jana Shikshana Nilayam's were established where ever there is accommodation and learners convenience were not taken into consideration while choosing the location of the centres.

TABLE - 3 LOCATION OF THE JSNS

S.No.	Place	Percentage
1.	Panchayat Office	42.00
2.	Prerak residence	35.00
3.	Temple	09.00
4.	School	07.00
5.	Houses of Learners and others	07.00

As JSNs were viewed as permanent institutions to cater to the needs of neo-literates particular and community as a whole, the programme administrators should take immediate and suitable steps to provide better and suitable housing facility for organisation of JSN activities successfully with effective participation of the community.

The enquiry regarding the location of JSNs discloses that the programme administrators has made ad-hock arrangement for housing of JSN. Further probe was made to identify the exact structure of the house. The probe reveals that the JSNs were located in Kacha houses (41%). Dabhas (26%), Hut (17%) and Puccka houses (16%) etc. This shows that location of JSNs were very poor, inadequate, not suitable and in convenient for arranging meetings with even 30 or ore adults. Certainly this type of arrangement may not be so attractive for the learners and community for attending frequent meetings.

TABLE-4: TYPE OF FACILITY AVAILABLE TO JSNS AND RESPECTIVE PERCENTAGES

S.No.	Type of house	Percentage
1.	Hut	17
2.	Kacha house	41
3.	Dabha	26
4.	Pucca house	16

In addition to the above, JSN should also perform the other functions viz. Library, Churcha mandal, dissemination of functional information, cultural and recreation activities, sports and games etc. Keeping in view of variety of activities, an enquiry into the timings and duration of organisation of JSN activities were also made and results were presented in the following pages.

ii. Timings of the Jana Shikshana Nilayam

The enquiry into the timing of the functioning of the Jana Shikshana Nilayams revealed that majority of the Jana Shikshana Nilayams were functioned during the night time. It is true that the cliental of the Jana Shikshana Nilayam were mostly peasants and they will be busy in cultivation during the day time. Due to this, they can spare some time only during night time and as a result, majority of the Jana Shikshana Nilayas were functioned during night time.

The results also reveals that the Jana Shikshana Nilayam were functioned during evening times (21%) and majority of them were functioned between 7 p.m. and 8 p.m. (52%) followed by 4 p.m. and 5 p.m. (13%) and 8 p.m. and 9 p.m. and per cent were from 6 p.m. to 7p.m.

TABLE-5: WORKING HOURS OF THE JANA SHIKSHANA NILAYAMS

S.No.	Duration	Percentage
1.	8 AM to 4 PM	2
2.	4 PM to 5 PM	13
3.	5 PM to 6 PM	2
4.	6 PM to 7 PM	6
5.	7 PM to 8 PM	53
6.	8 PM to 6 PM	13
7.	4 PM to 6 PM	4
8.	5 PM to 7 PM	1
9.	7 PM to 9 PM	1
10.	3 PM to 8 PM	1
11.	3 PM to 9 PM	4

The data also revealed that the duration of the functioning of the Jana Shikshana Nilayams were varied. Hence the Jana Shikshana Nilayams were reclassified keeping in view of the duration. The reclassification revealed that the Jana Shikshana Nilayams were organised only for one hour (89%) two hours (6%) and some were organised more than three hours (5%). The above findings clearly demonstrates that Jana Shikshana Nilayams were catering to the needs of people with different backgrounds. However uniformity cannot be imposed as scheme is more voluntary in nature.

TABLE-6: PERCENTAGE OF JSNS AS PER THE DURATION OF ACTIVITIES

S.No.	No. of Hours	Per cent
1.	One hour	87
2.	Two hours	6
3.	More than 3 hours	7

iii. Lighting Facilities

As most of the Jana Shikshana Nilayas were functioned during night time, these require adequate lighting equipment. Further, National Literacy Mission clearly, envisaged better and improvised lighting facilities to all the centres of adult education. It is also true that lighting facilities improves the quality of the programme. Keeping this in view, all the Jana Shikshana Nilayams were examined to identify the kind of lighting equipment that these Jana Shikshana Nilayams possessed. The information collected revealed (Table-7) the Jana Shikshana Nilayams (89%) were connected with electricity. Jana Shikshana Nilayams were also having more than one. The above information show that majority of Jana Shikshana Nilayams were having adequate lighting facilities. however, a few of them still does not have suitable lighting facilities. Hence, steps may be taken to provide at least petromax lights, where ever the electric facilities were not available.

TABLE-7 : LIGHTING FACILITIES

S.No.	Facility	Percentage
1.	Petromax	5
2.	Lantrine	2
3.	Electricity	89
4.	More than one of the above	4

iv. Furniture

It is rightly said that comfortable seating arrangements and pleasant environment attracts and retain the people. It is also true in the case of Jana Shikshana Nilayams. The enquiry with regard to the seating arrangements shows (Table-8) that 41 per cent of Jana Shikshana Nilayam were having table and chair for the preraks. Eighty one per cent of the Jana Shikshana Nilayams were having wooden planks and mats for learners. On the other hand 28 per cent of the Jana Shikshana Nilayams were not adequately equipped to perform its activities.

TABLE-8: FURNITURE AVAILABLE AT JSNS

S.No.	Type of the furniture	Percentage
1.	Wooden planks-mats	31
2.	Table & Chairs	41
3.	Almirah	28

Hence effects are required to provide similar facilities to all the JSNs so as to make the JSN a pleasurable place to spend the time and to over come the boredom of the routine day-to day life.

v. Book Keeping Facilities

The enquiry relating to the facilities to store books and transportation of books reveals that only 3 per cent of the Jana Shikshana Nilayams were having facilities to store the books and only seven per cent of the Jana Shikshana Nilayas were having cycle facility to visit the other villages for distribution and collection of books by the preraks.

TABLE-9 : BOOK KEEPING FACILITIES

S.No.	Faculty	Percentage
1.	Nil	97
2.	Trunk	2
3.	Woodenbox	1

TABLE-10: MEANS OF TRANSPORT FOR DISTRIBUTION OF BOOKS.

S.No.	Facility	Percentage
1.	Cycle	7
2.	By walk	93

The above enquiry clearly shows that the Jana Shikshana Nilayams were not having adequate facilities both for preraks, learners and storage facilities.

Inadequate physical facilities will hamper the efficiency of Jana Shikshana Nilayams. Hence, efforts has to be made to provide adequate setting arrangements and storage facilities, so as to make the stay of the learners in Jana Shikshana Nilayams were more pleasurable or otherwise participants certainly feel in-different and retaining the learners in the Jana Shikshana Nilayam will be a difficult job.

When enquired the adults about their preferential timing of organisation of Jana Shikshana Nilayams; the adults (36%) informed that they prefer night and 36 per cent evening (36%). Hence, Jana Shikshana Nilayam's should be organised according to the conveniences of the adults.

TABLE-11: TIMINGS PREFERRED BY THE ADULTS

S.No.	Timings	Percentage
1.	Evening	36
2.	Night	64

vi. Who are the Users of Jana Shikshana Nilayam

In order to find out whether the purpose for which the Jana Shikshana Nilayams were established were serving or not an enquiry was made to find out who is utilising the facilities of Jana Shikshana Nilayams and what proportion. It revealed that majority of them were adults, (93%). The further classification discloses that the users of JSNs were neo-literate (65%) and among them (64%) of them were adult learners. It clearly demonstrates that Jana Shikshana Nilayams were serving the purpose and were able to attract the target group.

Sum Up

The information presented in the previous pages on location, timing, duration, physical and infrastructural facilities available for JSNs discloses that majority of the JSNs were located at Panchayat offices and at Prerak residence. The location of the JSNs reveals that more than half of the JSNs were located at Kacha and Dabha houses. Very few of them were located in pucca houses. With regards to the timings, 87% of the JSNs were functioned for one hour in the night. Majority of the JSNs were electrified. One third of JSNs were having seating facility for learners and for preraks (41%). Storage facilities are very in-adequate. Transport facility for the preraks are very meagre.

SECTION - II

PERFORMANCE OF JANA SHIKSHANA NILAYAMS

i. Library

One of the important function of the Jana Shikshana Nilayams is to organise evening classes for providing promotion and consolidation of the literacy and prevention of adult neo-literates to relapse into illiteracy by creating learning environment and keeping available suitable reading materials. The regular use of reading materials not only enrich their literacy standard but also helps them to know the upto date knowledge in their profession. Ultimately this practice leads to the improvement of quality of life through positive out look towards current affairs, and tolerance.

Keeping inview of the importance of library activity in promotion and retention of literacy, an enquiry was made to find out its performance, in terms of the journals received, extent of utilisation of the reading materials, rate of return of the books to library, relevance of books to the needs of the people, physical facilities available etc and relevant data was collected and analysed. The findings were presented in the following pages.

TABLE-12: FACILITIES AVAILABLE FOR KEEPING THE BOOKS

S.No.	Facilities	Percentage
1.	Nil	97
2.	Trunk	2
3.	Wooden box	1

a. The Periodical Received

The enquiry revealed that all most all the JSN Libraries (94%) were received two dailies (Andhra Jyothi, Andhra Prabha) and Bala Jyothi (96%) a monthly magazine. Where as 5 and 7 per cent to the JSN libraries were received the Udayam and Enadu daily respectively.

The above information clearly shows that all the Jana Shikshana Nilayams were received the vernacular daily news papers and a children's Magazine (Bala Jyothi). Further, all the newspapers have allocated certain portion of the paper for the benefit of the neo-literates. The information provided in this Section mostly based on the needs of the community and was present in a simple and lucid language so as to enable the neo-literates to read and absorb the same with easy.

TABLE-13: PERIODICALS RECEIVED BY THE LIBRARY

S.No.	Periodicals	Percentage
1.	Eenadu	7
2.	Udayam	5
3.	Andhra Jyothi	94
4.	Andhra Prabha	94
5.	Bala Jyothi	96

b. Supply of Periodicals

Further enquiry was also made to identify whether the JSN Libraries were received the periodicals in-time or not. Surprisingly it revealed that 41 per cent of the Jana Shikshana Nilayams were not received the periodicals intime. It is understood that these Jana Shikshana Nilayam's were not received the periodicals directly but they were supplied indirectly through some other people. Hence, efforts should be made to identify the loop holes in this regard and administrators should take steps to see that the periodicals should reach the Library directly and also in-time.

TABLE-14: RECEIPT OF PERIODICALS BY JSNS IN TIME

S.No.	Category	Percentage
1.	Yes	59
2.	No	41

c. Utilisation of Periodicals and Books

The extent of the utilisation of the books and periodicals in the JSN Libraries disclosed that majority of the participants were using the materials more effectively (78 per cent) and effectively (14 per cent). However, 6 per cent of them felt that the Libraries were used and were assisted in creating favourable environment for nurturing the literacy among the neo-literates. The pattern of utilisation also shows that the neoliterates were used the books not only for strengthening their Literacy skills but also for acquiring the new information.

TABLE-15: EXTENT OF UTILISATION OF THE BOOKS

S.No.	Category	Percentage
1.	Very effectively	78
2.	Effectively	14
3.	Moderately	6
4.	Less effectively	1
5.	Very less effectively	1

d. Relevance of Books

After knowing the names of the periodicals, extent of utilisation and per cent of return of the books, further, Probe was also made to know the relevance of the books available in the Library to the target of the programme.

TABLE-16: RELEVANCE OF BOOKS TO THE NEEDS OF THE NEO-LITERATES

S.No.	Extent of relevance	Percentage
1.	Highly relevant	66
2.	Relevant	24
3.	Moderately	10

As per the preraks opinion it appears that 66 per cent of the books are extremely relevant and 24 per cent felt relevant and 10 per cent moderately useful. In other words the books supplied by the government to the Libraries and the books collected by the preraks from different sources were to the satisfaction of the neo-literates.

e. Return of the Books

The functioning of the Libraries not only depends on the extent of the utility and relevance of the books but also in the promotion of the healthy reading habits among the neo-literates. One of the good habits of using the Library is borrowing the books regularly and returning the books in-time to the library. When enquired about the extent of return of the books, it was found that only seven per cent of the neo-literates were not returned the books in time.

TABLE-17: EXTENT OF RETURN OF THE BOOKS

S.No.	Group	Percentage
1.	Less than 25	1
2.	26 to 50	6
3.	51 to 75	17
4.	76 and above	76

On the other hand 93 per cent of the learners were returned the books in time. The pattern of the return of the books clearly demonstrates that the neo-literates were visited the library and borrowed the books on regular basis.

f. Frequent Users of Library

The enquiry with regard to the regular and frequent users of Library, reveals that the frequent visitors of JSN Library were adults (33%) neo-literates (31%) Adult education learners (13%), school going children (11%) and other (12%). When sex was taken as criteria majority of the visitors were found to be women (58%) and men occupied with second position (47%). It may be due to the fact that men may be busy with bread earning activity and women after completing their house hold chores spending their leisure time at JSN Library. In other words women started utilising their leisure time fruit fully and it is a sign for their empowerment.

TABLE-18: FREQUENT USERS OF JSN LIBRARY

S.No.	Category	Percentage
1.	Adults	33
2.	Neo-literates	31
3.	Adult Education Learners	13
4.	Others	12
5.	School going children	11

TABLE-19: FREQUENT USERS ACCORDING TO SEX

S.No.	Group	Percentage
1.	Women	53
2.	Men	47

g. Facilities Available for Library

As described earlier, one of the important activity of the JSN is to maintain the Library and distribute the books in the hamlets affiliated to the JSN main village. In order to maintain the library and reading room at JSN and for distribution of books in the hamlets require certain infrastructural facilities and transport facilities. In other words efficient functioning of the Library depends on the facilities available at Library. Keeping this inview preraks were enquired about the facilities available at the library.

The enquiry revealed that non of the JSNs were having a separate reading room. Only 2 JSNs were possessed Trunk and one with wooden box for keeping the books. With regard to the transport facility for distribution of books only 3 preraks has their own cycles and rest of them (97%) were covering the hamlets by walk. In addition, the preraks were also enquired about the facilities that they have additionally created for the library. Ninty five per cent of the preraks informed that they have not created any extra facilities and only five per cent informed that they have created required additional facilities for the library. It appears that preraks were not able to generate extra facilities from the community. Hence, preraks must be encouraged to convince the community and obtain their support and participation in all literacy activities. From the above it appears that most of the Libraries were ill equipped and Physical facilities were very poor. In view of the above the performance of the Libraries may not be very encouraging.

ii. Organisation of Short-Term Programmes

One of the functions of the Jana Shikshana Nilayam's is to organise simple, short duration training programmes relating to the subjects such as health and family welfare, new developments in agriculture and animal husbandry, conservation of energy, improved Chulha etc. In addition Jana Shikshana Nilayam's should also to organise various vocational training programmes for the benefit of local youth. In otherwords the function of the Jana Shikshana Nilayams is not only to promote literacy but also to improve the functional skills as these will help to improve their Socio-economic conditions of the participation. Keeping inview of the importance of this role, preraks were requested to provide information about various short term courses conducted and extension lectures organised in co-operations with various development departments and extent of usefulness of the information available etc. The information thus collected were analysed and presented in the following pages.

a. Vocational Training Programmes

With regard to the Short term training programmes, the enquiry revealed that only two percent of the Jana Shikshana Nilayams have conducted the programme and 98 per cent have not organised any programmes. This shows that the performance of the Jana Shikshana Nilayams were very poor in this regard. Hence efforts should be made to encourage the preraks to organise functional development training programmes in different trades in co-operation with different agencies. Further, this type of activities inculcates confidence among the participants about the activities of Jana Shikshana Nilayam. Even if required, a separate training programme may be organised to the preraks so as to equip them in the above activities.

b. Extension Lectures

The Govt. has created a number of developmental departments to implement the various schemes/programmes formulated for the development of people. The information relating to the government programmes were not able to reach the target group as these were disseminated through selected channels only. In order to capture the latest information, Jana Shikshana Nilayams were supposed to organise extension lectures by inviting the officials of the development departments for the benefit of the neo-literates and community. However, in order to check whether the preraks have arranged extension lectures by inviting the experts to Jana Shikshana Nilayam to provide first hand information to the community, preraks were enquired and the obtained information were presented in the Table. 20.

Table. 20, shows that the Jana Shikshana Nilayams were arranged extension lectures on Health (79%), Animal Husbandry (71%), Agriculture (56%) and Family Welfare (57%). It appears that all the Jana Shikshana Nilayams invited the field experts of health, agriculture and Animal husbandry as these are the areas of immediate concern of community. In other words people were more concerned about their health and occupation. Hence it is advised that more information on different aspects of health and agriculture should be made available to the JSNs for wider dissemination among the community.

TABLE-20: TOPICS OF EXTENSION LECTURES

S.No.	Areas	Percentage
1.	Health	79
2.	Animal Husbandry	71
3.	Family Welfare	57
4.	Agriculture	56

The enquiry with regard to the availability of the resource persons in their respective villages shows that all the preraks of 100 villages informed that they don't have any resource person at their village. They also disclosed that they have not taken the villagers to any development department or to any agency. It clearly shows that these villages have to depend on outsiders for new information. Hence the developmental departments should take a lead to popularise the schemes by using all means so that these should reach the actual target group for effective use.

iii. JSN: An Information Window

The Government is implementing a number of welfare and developmental programmes for the benefit of the needy and poor. The success of these programmes depends in the effective utilisation and participation of target groups for whom these were formulated. The first step in this direction is the right sources for getting the upto date information. In this regard, the JSNs should act as an information window and should provide information on various developmental programmes and materials suitable for neo-literates. Keeping this inview, preraks were enquired about their sources of information on developmental programme. The findings reveals that half of the Jana Shikshana Nilayams were getting information from development departments (52%), followed by voluntary organisations (22%), Banks (18%), Business concerns (7%) and from social workers (1%).

TABLE-21: SOURCE OF INFORMATION ON DEVELOPMENTAL PROGRAMMES

S.No.	Source	Percentage
1.	Development Departments	52
2.	Banks	18
3.	Voluntary Organisations	22
4.	Business Concerns	7
5.	Social workers	1

The above clearly demonstrates that development departments themselves providing the information and acting as information centres. Further, it appears that the voluntary organisations were also playing a predominant role in disseminating information to the needy. Further, the banks which were responsible for providing credit facilities for the farmers in rural areas were found to have a cordial relationship with its target group by providing them the avenues and opportunities. On the whole the preraks were found to be active, able to contact a number of agencies for gathering the information and to popularise the same among the community so as to enable them to utilise the same for their advantage.

a. Utility of the Information Available

The above clearly demonstrates that development departments themselves providing the information and acting as major source of information for the community in the Jana Shikshana Nilayam. It is essential that the Prerak should explain to the community about the latest developments and encourage them to utilise the information for their occupational improvements.

The investigator collected the information with regard to the utility of the materials on developmental programmes at the Jana Shikshana Nilayam by the community and presented in the following pages.

From the table, its appears that one third of the preraks informed that the information was very effectively utilised by the community and 19 per cent felt that the information was effectively utilised. In other words half of the Jana Shikshana Nilayam's were effectively serving the needs of the community in the area of developmental information. Contrary to the above utility of the available information is moderate in case of 31 per cent of the Jana Sikshna Nilayams. However it also reveals that 16 per cent of the Jana Sikshna Nilayams were notable to utilise the information very effectively. On the whole it appears that only half of the Jana Sikshna Nilayams have functioned effectively. In this regard, and the other half may not be possessing or collecting the information suitable to the needs of the area. Hence, they should be encouraged to contact suitable agencies for collection of relevant information and the community may be motivated to utilise the same for their development.

TABLE-22: EXTENT OF UTILISATION OF INFORMATION

S.No.	Extent	Percentage
1.	Very effectively	34
2.	Effectively	19
3.	Moderately	31
4.	Less effectively	14
5.	Very less effectively	2
		100

iv. Organisation of Charcha Mandals

In order to encourage the community to participate in the developmental activities, the charcha mandals were envisaged as a part of JSN activities. The charcha mandal is nothing but a discussion group especially constituted for discussion of common problems of the community and to formulate strategies to over come the same thought the participation of the community. The enquiry in this regard reveals that only 41 per cent of the Jana Sikshna Nilayams were performing the role of organisation of charcha mandals, and rest of them could not organise. In other words, more than half of the JSNs were not able to organise the discussion groups. Hence preraks should be encourage to take lead in this direction as majority of the local problems can be solved by sitting together by all the concerned parties. Further, it also helps to curb the future problems at the budding stage it self.

TABLE-23 : ORGANISATION OF CHARCHA MANDALS

S.No.	No.	Percentage
1.	Yes	41
2.	No	59

a. Frequency of Meetings

The frequency of meeting of charcha mandal reveals that all the Jana Sikshna Nilayams have conducted one meeting per month and only one Jana Sikshna Nilayam have conducting more than one meeting.

TABLE-24: FREQUENCY OF CHARCHA MANDALS PER MONTH

S.No.	Frequency	Frequency
1.	One	40
2.	More than one time	1

This is an indication to say that people were often meeting together to discuss about their common concern and were able to take collective decisions. This process was not only created an opportunity for the community to sit together but also helping them to practice the democratic principles in solving their problems in a more mutually beneficial manner.

b. Topics Discussed

The topics discussed in the discussion group reveals that top priority was accorded to Health. The other aspects discussed were agriculture, Animal husbandry and family welfare. The pattern of topics chosen for discussion is an indication to say that the villagers were more concerned towards developmental issue than the domestic problems. Hence it appears that villages were of progressive in nature and does not reveal any unrest or tension.

TABLE-25: ASPECTS DISCUSSED AT CHARCHA MANDAL

S.No.	Items	Percentage
1.	Health	97
2.	Family Welfare	47
3.	Agriculture	48
4.	Agriculture	48

Implementation of Charcha Mandal Decisions

The decisions that were taken by the discussion groups in charcha mandals were implemented in all JSNs except in case of one Jana Shikshana Nilayam. It is true that they were able to solve the problem because these were related to the common causes and the decisions taken were unanimous with out my decent. The villages will progress if they were able to meet at frequent intervals and discuss the common issue.

TABLE-26: IMPLEMENTATION OF THE DECISIONS IN SOLVING THE PROBLEMS

S.No.	Category	Percentage
1.	Yes	97.56
2.	No	2.44

The above information reveals that the decisions taken at charcha mandals were implemented but it has not revealed the effectiveness felt by the community. Hence the further enquiry was made in this regard.

Effectiveness of the Implementation of Decisions

The information generated with regard to the effectiveness of the implementation of the decisions revealed that it as very effective (55 percentage) and effective (25%). Contrary to the above 15 per cent felt that the implementation of the decisions were less effective and very less effective (5%). In other words the decisions taken and implemented by the charcha mandal were not popular in the community.

TABLE-27: PROBLEM SOLVING EFFECTIVENESS

S.No.	Category	Percentage
1.	Very effectively	55
2.	Effectively	25
3.	Moderately	0
4.	Less effectively	15
5.	Very Less effectively	5

a. Charcha Mandal for Women

Though half of our population were women they were not allowed to participate in social, economic development activities and in all spears of life due to the traditions and superstitious beliefs. Further their opinions were not reflected in the decisions taken at the family level in specific and community as a whole. However, in view of the empowerment of women due to the literacy programmes and exposure to the mass media an enquiry was made whether a separate charcha mandal was organised or not for the women.

TABLE-27: JSNS WITH SEPARATE CHARCHA MANDAL FOR WOMEN

S.No.	Category	Percentage
1.	Yes	5
2.	No	95

The information generated revealed that only five per cent of the Jana Shikshana Nilayams were conducted separate discussion group for women and in case of 95 per cent JSNs women have participated along with the men. The trend is encouraging however after some time it is better to have separate charcha mandals for women so that they can express their concern and opinions with out any inhibition and hesitations. Incase of mixed groups women may feel hesitant to discuss the aspects concerned with women.

b. Participation of People in the Charcha Mandals

The success of the charcha mandals closely associated with the extent of the participation of the community in it. An enquiry was made to seek information about the community involvement in discussion group and the information collected was presented in the following table.

TABLE-29: EXTENT OF PEOPLES PARTICIPATION IN CHARCHA MANDALS

S.No.	Category	Percentage
1.	Very effective	87
2.	Effective	2
3.	Moderate	2
4.	Less effective	4
5.	Very less effective	5

The above table discloses that 89 per cent of the preraks were able to generate the effective participation of the community in charcha mandals and only two per cent of preraks felt that people participation is moderate. Contrary to the above nine per cent of the preraks informed that participation of the community is negligible. Hence, effort should be made to enthuse the community through preraks to participate in the discussion groups so as to achieve the community harmony and integration.

v. Sports and Adventurous Activities

One of the role of the Jana Shikshana Nilayam is to organise games and sports in the villages coming under its jurisdiction. The aim of this activity is to bring team spirit integration and communal harmony among various sections of the community.

The enquiry about the games & sports conducted at the Jana Shikshana Nilayam, revealed that Kabadi, Football, volley ball, Tenny cait caroms and chess were found to be popular and were organised at regular intervals. The pattern of the games shows that only few categories of games and sports have organised and they could not organise more varieties due to lack of physical facilities and materials. However when enquired about the additional facilities created, all the preraks (except three) informed that they have created additional facilities for organising these games. In other words the infrastructural facilities for promotion of games and sports created by the programme administration were not sufficient. It is also true that most of the villages does not have such facilities.

TABLE-30: GAMES AND SPORTS ORGANISED AT JSNS

S.No.	Games	Percentage
1.	Kabadi	96
2.	Foot ball	85
3.	Volley-ball	68
4.	Tenny coit	60
5.	Caroms	50
6.	Chess	41

a. Sports Material Available at Jana Shikshana Nilayam

Keeping in view of the above finding, further enquiry was also made to identify the sports material available at Jana Shikshana Nilayams. It was found that 87 per cent of the Jana Shikshana Nilayams were possessed foot ball, Tenny coit (73%), Chess (72%) and Caroms (51%). In other words majority of the Jana Shikshana Nilayams were having only 3 types of sports materials. As a result they were not able to expose themselves for other sports and games.

TABLE-31: SPORTS MATERIAL AVAILABLE AT JSNS

S.No.	Materials	Percentage
1.	Foot ball	88
2.	Tenny coit (Ringball)	73
3.	Chess Board	72
4.	Caroms	51

b. Utility of Games and Sports Materials

The utility of the available games and sports materials revealed that these materials were effectively (28%) and moderately (24%) utilised. Contrary to the above 48 per cent, nearly half of the preraks felt that they were not very useful. In other words the materials supplied either may be defective or they may not be liked by the community. Probably this may be the one of the reasons why the preraks informed that they have created infrastructure and other facilities to organise the games and sports.

TABLE-32: UTILITY OF SPORTS AND GAMES MATERIALS

S.No.	Extent of usefulness	Percentage
1.	Highly useful	5
2.	Useful	23
3.	Moderately useful	24
4.	Less useful	32
5.	Not fully useful	16

c. Women Participation in Games and Sports

One of the major objectives of the Jana Shikshana Nilayam's is to create the awareness among women about their status and to motivate them to participate effectively in all spears of life to lead a more meaningful life by enjoying their rightful share. Participation in Games and Sports by the women leads to not only to reduce their day-today tensions but also promotes the group cohesiveness among the community.

Keeping this inview, the preraks were asked to identify the games and sports in which women have shown interest and extent of their participation in them.

The findings reveals that women were fond of playing tenny coit (98 per cent) throw ball (58%) and chess (65%).

TABLE-33: PARTICIPATION OF WOMEN IN GAMES & SPORTS

S.No.	Name of the Game	Percentage
1.	Ring	98
2.	Chess	65
3.	Throw ball	58

d. Extent of Participation

The extent of participation of women in the sports & games, revealed that 15 per cent of them were found to be effectively participated and 32 per cent of them were moderately participated. Contrary to the above 54 per cent, i.e., more than half of them have participated less effectively. In other words half of the women were participated in the games and sports half-heartedly or by force. Its may also be due to lack of interest or personal reasons. Hence, it is necessary to identify the reasons for not effective participation of the women in the sports and games and these may be organised based on their interests.

TABLE-34: EXTENT OF PARTICIPATION OF WOMEN IN SPORTS & GAMES

S.No.	Extent	Percentage
1.	Very Less	21
2.	Less	32
3.	Moderate	32
4.	High	14
5.	Very high	1

vi. Cultural and Entertainment Programmes Publicity of Jana Shikshana Nilayam Activities

For successful implementation of any mass programme requires effective publicity and propaganda not only to inform the community about the aims and objectives of the programme but also how this can be utilise by them. This is also true in the case of Jana Shikshana Nilayams. Keeping this inview, when enquired about the means and media used for propagation of the activities of the Jana Shikshana Nilayams it is was found that 44% of the Jana Shikshana Nilayams have organised cycle realise in the village, 40 per cent of them propagated through literacy songs and dramas highlighting the importance of literacy and activities of the Jana Shikshana Nilayams. On the other hand 14 per cent of the

Jana Shikshana Nilayams through songs and burrakathas and two per cent of them through propaganda.

TABLE-35: MEANS OF PROPAGATION OF JSNS

S.No.	Activity	Percentage
1.	Cycle Rally	44
2.	Literacy Dramas	40
3.	Literacy Songs	12
4.	Propaganda	2
5.	Burrakatha	2

The above findings clearly demonstrates that not adequate publicity was given to Jana Shikshana Nilayams through more meaningful and effective means at village level. Hence, it is the opinion of the investigator that lack of publicity is the main reason for not so success of the Jana Shikshana Nilayams. Hence it is the high time to redraft the publicity agenda of the Jana Shikshana Nilayam's by revitalising the literacy committees at the village level.

vii. Community Co-operation in Learning Activities

Community co-operation is a pre-condition for organising any activity at the village level especially this is so incase of adult education activities. The enquiry reveals that majority of the preraks reported that they have received a very good responsive (57%) good (8%) and moderate (15%) co-operation in organising Jana Shikshana Nilayams activities.

TABLE-36: COMMUNITY COOPERATION

S.No.	Category	Percentage
1.	Very good	57
2.	Good	18
3.	Moderate	15
4.	Low	6
5.	Very Low	4

Contrary to the above only 10 percent of the preraks feel that they were not able to secure any co-operation from the community. Though this is very small but efforts must be made to train the preraks in skills of obtaining co-operation or the local leader should be consulted and obstacle may be removed in securing effective co-operation from the community.

viii. Classification of JSNs

In order to classify the JSNs based on their performance of various roles, suitable numerical values were assigned to them to measure their extent of the performance on all the identified functions. The mean value of JSN performance were arrived and JSNs were categorised based on the criterion mean ± 1/2 SD and results were presented in the following table.

TABLE 37: EXTENT OF THE PERFORMANCE OF THE JSNS

S.No.	Level of Performance	N	Mean
1.	Poor	27	< 131.23
2.	Average	36	131.24 to 139.23
3.	Good	37	193.24 >

The results presented in the above table clearly demonstrates that more than two thirds of the JSNs were found to be effectively performing their role. On the other hand 27% are poor in their performance. Hence, steps should be taken to improve the performance of the poorly performed JSNs.

SECTION - III

PROFILE OF WORKING PRERAKS

The major functions of the Jana Shikshana Nilayams are to organise evening literacy classes, library, charcha mandal, short-terms vocational training programmes, sports and cultural activities, and act as a communication window for information relating to the developmental programmes. In orders to make the Jana Shikshana Nilayams as popular institution among the community and to manage its activities, a post of prerak was created. The prerak was expected to conduct activities of a Jana Shikshana Nilayams with the help of volunteers in the villages other than the ones in which the Jana Shikshana Nilayams is situated. Prerak is also expected to carry the newspapers, journals and books at the time of his visit to the affiliated villages and organise inter village sports and cultural competitions.

The guidelines on Jana Shikshana Nilayam prescribed certain qualities and qualifications for the prerak as he/she is the back bone for the entire scheme. As per the Jana Shikshana Nilayam guidelines prerak should possess: Interest in serving the community, particularly women and economically deprived sections of the society; leadership qualities and ability, static voluntary help of the local youth; free time, at least 3-4 hours once a week, matriculation qualification to be reduced to VIIth class level in case of specially gifted persons, women and person belonging to SC/ST etc. It is clear from the above that the policy makers have taken at most care while formulating he guidelines in assigning the roles and functions to the Jana Shikshana Nilayam's and as well as qualities required for the preraks. In other words prerak should be an effective person.

In the light of the above, the personal traits of the working preraks were analysed to bring out the salient features of the working preraks.

The data relating to the background information of preraks were presented in the table 38.

From the table 38 it is evident that majority of the selected preraks were men. Only around one third of them were women. Caste wise classification reveals that majority of the preraks were belongs to un-previlized sections. it is a positive trend as majority of the illiterates were also from the same sections. Age wise distribution also shows that the majority of the preraks belongs to younger age group and only 23 per cent of them were having more than 31 years of age. An equal number of the preraks (42 per cent) were having less than Rs. 5,000/- and five to ten thousand rupees of income per annum and only 16 per cent of them are having more than ten thousand income. In other words majority of the preraks were from lower middle class families.

Occupation point of view 45 per cent of them were agriculture coolies and 28 per cent of them agriculturists. On the other hand rest of them were from the areas of business and coolies.

When marriage was taken as criteria 56 per cent of them were married and rest of them not married (44%). Similarly, experience in adult education shows that 54 per cent of them were having 3 to 5 years of experience in the field of adult education. It implies that preference was given to those having experience in the field adult education while selecting the preraks.

The classification of the preraks based on their education level, it clearly demonstrates that only 11 per cent of the working preraks possessed inter and less educational qualification and rest of the preraks were graduates and post-graduates. In other words preraks were well educated.

On the whole majority of the working preraks were men younger in age-group belongs to unpreviliged sections with lower middle class families, with agriculture background, married, with high level of education and less than two years of experience in the field of adult education. In other words, majority of the working preraks were from the similar background that of the participants of adult education.

In order to identify the profile of an effective preraks, the working preraks were categorised into different groups based on their characteristics. Further the preraks were also categorised into three groups based on their obtained mean effectiveness scores by following the criteria mean effectiveness score ± ½ SD. The x^2 test was applied to find out the association between the personal characteristics and the prerak effectiveness. The influence of the personal variable on the prerak effectiveness was also identified. The findings of the above analysis was presented in the following pages.

i. Association Between Personal Variables and Prerak Effectiveness

The findings presented in the table 37 with regard to the association between the prerak characteristics viz., sex, caste, occupation, income, experience, education, marital status, age and attitude and prerak effectiveness discloses that the association is significant only in case of the variable 'caste'. It clearly demonstrates that caste is closely associated with prerak effectiveness.

TABLE-38: DISTRIBUTION OF CHI-VALUES IN RESPECT OF PERSONAL VARIABLES AND PRERAK EFFECTIVENESS

S.No.	Variable	DF	Chi-value
1.	Sex	2	1.02@
2.	Caste	4	7.42*
3.	Occupation	4	1.85@
4.	Income	4	6.35@
5.	Experience	4	1.02@
6.	Education	2	1.05@

{Cont.}.....

7.	Marital Status	2	4.53@
8.	Age	4	0.89@
9.	Attitude	4	5.43@

@ not significant * Significant at 0.05 level

ii. Influence of the Personal Characteristics of the Preraks on Prerak Effectiveness

The findings presented in the table with regard to the influence of the personal characteristics of the preraks on prerak effectiveness discloses the following.

1. Sex versus prerak effectiveness

The obtained mean effectiveness score of the men and women preraks shows that women were found to be more effective than the men preraks. however the calculated 't' reveals that the difference between the two groups is statistically not significant.

2. Caste versus prerak effectiveness

The prerak effectiveness scores obtained by the preraks belonging to three caste groups disclosed that the preraks from forward caste group have scored more mean effectiveness followed by BC and SC/ST preraks. However the three groups of preraks does not differ significantly from each other.

3. Occupation versus prerak effectiveness

The trend of the obtained prerak effectiveness scores of the agriculturists, labourers and others group of preraks disclosed that preraks with labour background was found to be more effective preraks and preraks with other occupational group have scored very low effectiveness scores. However again three groups of preraks does not differ significantly from each other.

4. Income versus prerak effectiveness

. The results presented in the table 39 revealed that preraks with more income group proved to be more effective preraks than the middle and low income groups. This is probably due to the fact that the more income groups may be more educated and have more awareness and as a result they might have performed well as preraks.

5. Experience versus prerak effectiveness

The influence of the experience of the preraks demonstrates that more experience group of preraks have proved to be more effective preraks than the less experienced in adult education. More experienced may be able to attract the adults better and may be in a position to organise the activities in a better manner.

4. Education versus prerak effectiveness

The findings presented in the table with regard to the influence of education on prerak effectiveness shows that more educated preraks were proved to be more effective than the low educated preraks. However the difference between these two groups was not statistically significant.

5. Marital status versus prerak effectiveness

The results relating to the influence of marital status on prerak effectiveness disclosed that the married preraks were found to be more effective preraks than the un-married preraks but it is not statistically supported by the obtained 't' value.

6. Age verses prerak effectiveness

The obtained mean effectiveness scores of the preraks belonging to different age groups showed that preraks with more age were found to be more effective followed by middle and young age group of preraks. However the calculated 't' value was not significant.

7. Attitude versus prerak effectiveness

In order to study the relationship between attitude and prerak effectiveness, the preraks were categories into three groups based on their obtained attitudes scores and studied differences in terms of their effectiveness scores. The obtained mean effectiveness scores of these three groups shows that preraks with more positive attitude towards various aspects of JSN were found to be more popular followed by medium and low attitude groups.

SUM UP

iii. Characteristics of an Effective Prerak

From the above it can be assumed that preraks belonging to the women, forward caste, labourers, more income, more experienced, more educated, married, elders, more positive attitude groups were proved to be more effective preraks. Hence it is suggested while selecting the preraks above may be kept in view for effective implementation of the scheme of Jana Shikshana Nilayam's.

TABLE-39: MEAN EFFECTIVENESS, SD'S AND T/F VALUES OBTAINED BY PRERAKS BELONGING TO DIFFERENT GROUPS

S.No.	Variable	Group	N	Mean effective-ness score	S.D.	t/F
1.	Sex	Men	70	134.81	25.16	1.49@
	Women	30	148.20	27.29		
2.	Caste	SC/ST	35	133.14	34.04	0.07@
	BC	38	138.81	18.73		
	OC	27	140.66	22.69		
3.	Occupation	Agriculture	28	125.35	34.79	1.11@
	Labours	27	134.14	34.89		
	Others	45	115.60	30.15		
4.	Income	Low	42	133.30	26.30	1.38@
	Middle	19	135.31	26.49		
	More	39	142.64	25.08		
5.	Experience	Less	54	130.30	26.30	1.38@
	More	46	134.23	26.49		
6.	Education	Low	70	134.81	25.85	1.22@
	More	30	143.67	24.51		
7.	Marital	Married	57	140.08	25.89	0.73@
	Status	Unmarried	43	133.67	24.51	
8.	Age	Young	35	133.14	34.04	0.73@
	Middle	38	138.81	18.73		
	Elders	27	140.66	22.69		

{Cont.}.........

9.	Attitude	Low	35	133.86	27.74	1.68@
		Medium	34	135.88	20.01	
		More	31	136.26	26.60	

@ not significant

SECTION IV

READING INTERESTS OF THE NEO-LITERATES

In order to identify the reading interests of the neo-literates the collected data was pooled, analysed and classified the reading interests into three categories viz, more popular, popular and less popular by using the criteria Mean ± ½ SD. As per this criteria, the reading interest items having mean 3.80 and more were treated as more popular reading interests items falling between 3.79 and 3.41 as popular and less than 3.41 as less popular. Based on this criteria out of 147 items, 76 were found to be more popular, 40 popular and remaining 31 less popular reading interests. In other words half of the items included in the inventory were preferred by the majority of the sample neo-literate as more popular reading interests. These reading interest items mostly belongs to the areas of health, family, social matters, agriculture, mythology, religion and industry & economy. The list of the more popular reading interests/items were shown below.

TABLE-40: MORE POPULAR READING INTEREST ITEMS AND THEIR RESPECTIVE MEAN VALUES AS PREFERRED BY THE TOTAL SAMPLE NEO-LITERATE

Sl. No.	More popular reading interest items	Mean value
1.	National flag and song	4.51
2.	High yielding groundnut cultivation	4.40
3.	Life stories of freedom fighters	4.38
4.	Health air	4.37
5.	Clean surroundings	4.36
6.	Clean water	4.35
7.	Developed variety of fruit cultivation	4.32
8.	Education facilities for children	4.31
9.	Village cleanliness and health	4.29
10.	High yielding vegetable cultivation	4.28
11.	Hygienic house	4.27
12.	Flower cultivation	4.28
13.	Family income and savings	4.23
14.	First-aid	4.22
15.	Family health	4.21

{Cont.}...

16.	Ramayana	4.21
17.	Our country's independence	4.20
18.	Use of social forestry	4.16
19.	We and our environment	4.16
20.	Use of social forestry	4.15
21.	Moral stories	4.14
22.	Utility of adult franchise	4.14
23.	Religious places of our country	4.12
24.	Care of our body	4.12
25.	Control of mosquito and housefly	4.11
26.	Small family-economic development	4.11
27.	Rights and duties of a citizen	4.10
28.	Family planning	4.10
29.	Children's health and vaccination	4.10
30.	Mahabharata	4.09
31.	Common diseases	4.08
32.	Eradication of dowry system	4.07
33.	Primary health centre	4.05
34.	Ornament and other materials in gold and silver	4.05
35.	Care of pregnant women	4.05
36.	Legal protection for labourers	4.05
37.	Eradication of untouchability	4.05
38.	Vaccination	4.03
39.	U.N.O. and world peace	4.03
40.	Diseases and insects in crops and their removal	4.01
41.	High yielding paddy cultivation	4.01
42.	Television programmes	4.01
43.	Diseases and necessary treatment	4.00
44.	Balanced diet	4.00
45.	Women's rights	3.98
46.	Kindness towards creatures	3.97
47.	Food preservation methods	3.97
48.	High yielding bajra cultivation	3.97
49.	Child care	3.95
50.	Protection of crops from mouse	3.95
51.	Improved agricultural instruments	3.95
52.	Yoga and exercise	3.95
53.	Preservation of crops and seeds	3.93
54.	Merits of life insurance	3.93
55.	Tailoring	3.93
56.	Different kinds of manure and its application	3.92
57.	Responsibilities and duties of public health worker	3.91
58.	Non-formal education	3.90
59.	Hinduism	3.89
60.	Preparation of land for different types of cultivation	3.89
61.	Krishnavatharam	3.88
62.	Srimad Bhagavad Gita	3.88
63.	Radio programmes	3.88
64.	Modern irrigation methods	3.88
65.	Patriotic leaders	3.88
66.	Different facilities for family welfare	3.88

{Cont.}.......

67.	Suitable occupation for welfare	3.87
68.	Small savings scheme	3.87
69.	Women welfare programmes	3.87
70.	Voluntary organisations and functions	3.86
71.	Stories	3.84
72.	Cottage industries	3.82
73.	Disinfection of seeds	3.80
74.	Buddudu	3.80
75.	Toy and other material in wood	3.80

In view of the above while preparing neo-literate literature, the items found to be more popular among the neo-literate should be considered. Further efforts should be made to popularise these items among the authors and publishers who were involved in the adult education field so that they can concentrate on these issues and bring out more attractive and relevant materials. Once the reading materials on interesting aspects are available, the neo-literate will certainly utilise their reading skills to read these materials. Constant use of their skills certainly helps them to enhance their allround development. With regard to the popular and less popular items, it appears that only a small group of neo-literates have checked the above items as their reading interests. Hence less priority may be given while publishing general reading materials to the above items. However, wherever situation specific materialise are needed, the above aspects may also be considered.

Neo-Literate Literature Supplied to JSNs

In order to asses the relevance of the literature supplied to the JSNs to the reading interests of the neo-literate, the list of the titles of the books supplied to the JSNs of the 4 districts were collected. To the surprise of the investigator all the JSNs were having same titles with multiple copies. On enquiry it was learnt that, the state Directorate of Adult Education has supplied a list of the approved titles and firms, and the concern project officers were expected to choose the relevant title suitable to the needs of the area and interests of the neo-literate. As the list of the titles supplied by the Directorate is too small and there is no alternative for the programme staff, they have ordered almost all books that was listed. The titles supplied to the JSNs were from the areas of health & family social matters., agriculture, mythology, religion, industry and economy.

A glance into the list of popular reading interests identified and the list of the titles supplied to JSNs reveals that the books supplied to the JSNs were closely related to the reading interests of the neo-literate. Hence the hypothesis "The effective functioning of the JSN's depends on the availability of the suitable reading materials" is accepted. Probably, it may be the one of the reasons for regular use of books by the neo-literate and making frequent visits to the JSN's. Hence, it is advised that more relevant books may be supplied to the JSNs so as to promote the regular reading interest habits among the neo-literate.

SECTION - V

FACTORS INFLUENCING THE JSN PERFORMANCE

JSNs were created to promote, strengthen and consolidate the literacy among the neo-literates and to empower them through various activities inside the JSN and in the community as a whole. In order to perform the various functions of the JSNs, the JSNs were manned by a prerak. The prerak is the key for organisation of various activities of the JSNs with the active cooperation and participation of the community. In other words, the performance of the JSNs largely depends on the preraks, community, and the infrastructures available at the JSNs. Inview of the above, it is assumed that the factors relating to the above plays a significant role in determining the effectiveness of the JSNs. Hence this section analyses the influence of the infrastructure, prerak effectiveness, prerak problems, prerak attitude, community attitude and community support on the performance of the JSNs.

i. Infrastructure Vs JSN Performance

In order to facilitate the functioning of JSNs certain infrastructure was create by the programme administrators and community also supplemented for the same. It is but natural that JSNs with better infrastructural facilities will attract and retain the adults in the JSNs. Keeping this inview information relating to the infrastructural facilities available at JSNs was collected and quantified. Based on the quantified score of infrastructural facilities, JSNs were classified into three categories by following the criterion of mean ± 1/2 S.D. and related performance scores of the JSNs were calculated. The table 41 presents the mean JSN performance scores, SDs and obtained 'F' values by the JSNs with low medium and well equipped in terms of infrastructure.

TABLE-41: MEAN PERFORMANCE SCORES, SDS AND OBTAINED ANOVA VALUES OF THE JSNS WITH DIFFERENT INFRASTRUCTURAL FACILITIES.

S.No.	Infrastructural Level	N	Mean	SD	F
1.	Low	28	127.86	6.84	
2.	Medium	47	136.13	5.85	34.09*
3.	High	25	142.04	6.54	

*significant

From the above it is clear that out of hundred JSNs twenty five were found to be well equipped followed by 47 moderately equipped and 28 were found to be less equipped. The mean performance of the JSNs also shows that well equipped JSNs have obtained better performance scores. Further the trend of the mean performance scores also reveals that there is a relationship between performance and infrastructural facilities available at JSNs. In addition the obtained 'F' value was also found to be significant at 0.01 level. In view of the above the hypothesis "the availability of the proper infrastructure is likely to enhance the functioning of the JSNs" is accepted. Hence, in order to enhance the performance of the JSNs all the JSNs should be equipped adequately.

ii. Prerak Effectiveness Vs JSN Performance

In order to identify the influence of the prerak effectiveness on JSN performance, the monitors were classified into three groups based on the criteria mean effectiveness score ± ½ SD and ANOVA test was applied. The classification of the prerak effectiveness scores revealed that the difference between the less, moderately and more effective preraks performance in terms of JSN effectiveness is considerably very less. However, the trends of the obtained mean effectiveness scores reveals that the JSNs organised by the more effective preraks were found to more effective than the less effective preraks. In view of the above, the hypothesis "The effective functioning of the JSNs depends on the degree of the effectiveness of the preraks" was not accepted. However, the trend of the effectiveness scores revealed that the JSN efficiency always go's with the efficiency of the preraks.

iii. Prerak Attitude Vs JSN Performance

The successful functioning of any educational programmes largely depends on the attitude of its functionaries towards the various aspects of the programme. This is also true incase of the JSNs, keeping this inview, based on the attitude scores, the preraks were classified into three groups based on the criteria Mean ± ½ SD and respective JSN effectiveness scores were calculated for the three groups. The ANOVA Test was applied to find out the differences if any between the three groups. The results presented in the table discloses that the ANOVA value is not significant. It appears that the performance of the JSNs organised by the preraks with different levels of attitude is statistically similar. In view of the above results, the hypotheses "Positive attitude of preraks towards various aspects of JSN leads to the effective functioning of JSNs" is not accepted.

TABLE-42: MEAN JSN EFFECTIVENESS, SD, AND OBTAINED 'F' VALUE BY THE LESS, MODERATE AND MORE EFFECTIVE PRERAKS.

S.No.	Level of Effectiveness	N	Mean	SD	'F'
1.	Less	31	134.68	9.49	
2.	Moderate	34	134.41	8.94	0.79@
3.	More	35	136.68	5.79	

@ Not significant

TABLE-43: MEAN JSN EFFECTIVENESS SCORES, SDS OBTAINED ANOVA VALUE BY THE PRERAKS WITH DIFFERENT LEVELS OF ATTITUDE.

S.No.	Level of attitude	N	Mean	SD	ANOVA
1.	Low	35	133.86	8.57	
2.	Medium	34	135.88	8.86	0.84@
3.	High	31	136.26	6.78	

@ Not significant

However, the trend of the obtained mean effectiveness scores shows that higher the positive attitude of the preraks higher will be the effectiveness of the JSN. Hence curriculum for the pre-service and in-service training programmes for the preraks may be restructured to include the items relating to the building of attitude and attitudinal modifications. Such training and constant interaction with programme implementors will change the attitude of the preraks in desired direction.

iv. Prerak Problems Vs JSN Performances

The prerak in-charge of JSN is expected to perform a number of roles both in side and out side the JSN. As a result of the multiple roles to be performed by the prerak, he/she is supposed to interact with a good number of people with different background and out looks. As a result of this, certainly preraks has to face a number of problems in their day-today activities.

It is possible that due to the constant exposure of preraks to the simple problems in their day-today activities of the JSN, the performance of the JSN is likely to suffer. Keeping this in view, the problem scale was administered to all the selected preraks, relevant data was collected and analysed. The preraks were classified into three groups based on the criteria Mean problem score ± ½ SD and their respective JSN effectiveness scores were calculated. The mean JSN effectiveness scores, SDs and obtained 'F' values of the preraks belonging to less, moderate and more problems were presented in the table 44.

TABLE-44: MEAN JSN EFFECTIVENESS, SDS AND OBTAINED ANOVA VALUE BY THE PRERAKS WITH LESS, MODERATE AND MORE PROBLEMS.

S.No.	Extent of problems	N	Mean	SD	F
1.	Less	18	134.61	8.64	
2.	Moderate	79	135.53	7.99	0.21@
3.	More	3	133.00	12.28	

@ Not significant

The findings presented in the table discloses that majority of the preraks were of moderate problem group (69%) followed by less problem group (18%). However, a few preraks (13%) were belongs to more problem group. The trend of the obtained mean JSN effectiveness scores of the 3 groups reveales that moderate problem group of preraks were found to be organising the JSNs effectively than the other groups. However the calculated 'F' value not significant and hence the hypothesis "Lesser the problems faced by the preraks in organising JSN higher will be the effective functioning of JSN" is not accepted in toto. However from the above, majority of the preraks were found to be performing their roles effectively inspite of the problems that they were encountered in organising the JSNs.

v. Community Support Vs JSN Performance

As the JSNs were created for the benefit of the neo-literates in particular and the community as a whole, the success of the JSNs largely lies in the participation and support provided by the community in all its activities. Hence an attempt was made to identify the extent of the support received and its impact on the effectiveness of the JSN. As a first step in this direction, the JSNs were classified into three groups viz. more, moderate and less support enjoyed by the JSNs from the community based on the obtained community support scores and their respective JSN effective scores were calculated. The mean JSN effectiveness score, SDs and obtained 'F' value by the JSNs with more, moderate and less support enjoyed from the community was presented in the table 45.

TABLE-45: MEAN JSN EFFECTIVENESS, SDS AND OBTAINED ANOVA VALUES BY THE PRERAKS WITH DIFFERENT LEVELS OF COMMUNITY SUPPORT.

S.No.	Extent of support	N	Mean	SD	F
1.	More	21	137.95	39.51	
2.	Moderate	48	109.25	26.36	1.06@
3.	Less	31	113.97	31.66	

@ Not significant

The finding presented in the above table discloses that the calculated 'F' value between the three groups of JSNs found to be not significant. Hence the hypothesis. "The effective function of the JSN depends on the degree of the support received from the community" was not accepted. However the trend of the obtained mean effectiveness scores of JSNs shows that the JSNs which enjoyed more support from the community was found to be more effective than the other two groups. On the other hand the JSNs with low community support was also found to be more effective than the JSNs with moderate community support. In other words it appears that community support also effect the effectiveness of the JSNs. In view of the above, the programme administrators should take steps for promoting the community support to the various activities of the JSNs by involving them at all stages of the programme implementation.

vi. Community Attitude Vs JSN Performance

One of the important functions of JSNs is to create learning society and to provide relevant information to the community for utilising the Govt. sponsored programmes for their upliftment. In other words, JSNs should perform different roles within and out side the JSNs. The effective performance of various roles outside the JSNs largely governed by the community attitudes towards it. If community is satisfied with regard to JSN activities then the JSN will become a popular institution among the community. Keeping this in view the community attitude towards various activities of the JSN was measured and classified the JSNs into three categories namely low, medium and high attitude groups based on the criteria mean ± 1/2 S.D. and corresponding the JSN performance scores were also calculated for the above three groups and presented in the table 46 The table presents the mean JSN effectiveness scores, SDs and obtained 'F' values by the JSNs with low, medium and high community attitudes scores.

TABLE-46 MEAN JSN EFFECTIVENESS, SDS AND OBTAINED 'F' VALUE BY THE COMMUNITY WITH DIFFERENT LEVELS OF ATTITUDE.

S.No.	Level of community attitude	N	Mean	SD	F
1.	Low	33	133.97	8.84	
2.	Medium	39	136.05	8.83	0.65@
3.	High	28	135.79	6.19	

@ Not significant

The results presented in the above table clearly demonstrate that the difference between the mean JSN effectiveness scores obtained by three groups of JSNs with different levels of community attitude does not differ significantly with each other. However the obtained mean JSN effectiveness scores disclosed that higher the positive attitude of the community, better the performance of the JSNs. hence it is always better to create positive attitude among the community towards the various activities of the JSNs for its successful implementation. However the hypothesis" the positive attitude of the community towards the JSN is closely related with its effective functioning" is rejected as the calculated 'F' value were found to be not significant.

SUM UP

The findings presented in the previous pages with regard to the factors influencing the JSN performance clearly reveals that infrastructure of the JSN is closely related to the performance of the JSN. However the obtained mean performance scores of different factors reveals that effectiveness of the prerak, positive attitude, less problems, positive community attitude and more community support will have a say on the performance of the JSNs.

5

SUMMARY AND CONCLUSIONS

Literacy is one of the key aspects for human resource development. In order to qualify human resources of the country, the Govt of India has launched a number of Adult Education programmes for the promotion of literacy. As a result, a large pool of newly made literates were created. In order to prevent them to relapse into illiteracy and to institutionalise the post-literacy programme, the scheme of Jana Shikshana Nilayams were launched through out the country.

The major objectives of the JSN is to provide facilities for retention, continuing education and application of functional literacy, dissemination of information, creation of awareness about National concerns among the community, to improve the productivity etc. Each JSN is headed by a prerak and is expected to cover a cluster of 4 to 5 villages with a population of about 5,000. As per the scheme of JSN it is expected to organise an evening class for up gradation of literacy skills, maintain a library with a separate reading room, organises a charcha mandal, conducts a simple, short duration of training programs, organise games and sports, acts as an information window and communication centre. In addition it should also organise recreational and cultural activities.

In view of the above the JSNs should perform a number of functions not only for retention of literacy but also to accelerate the socio-economic development of the country. Hence it is necessary to have the knowledge of the activities that were undertaken inside the JSN and in the community. This will go in a long way in formulating effective strategies for improving quality of the programme and to modify the various aspects suitable to the local conditions.

A review of the already available literature reveals that very few studies have been under taken and the findings of the studies does not reveal the clear picture of the JSNs. Hence the present study was undertaken not only to assess, the functioning of the JSNs but also to identify the factors contributing for its success. To be specific the objectives of the study are as follows.

i. To measure the effectiveness of JSN based on its performance of various activities.

ii. To find out the availability of infrastructure for the organisation of JSNs.

iii. To ascertain the community attitude towards the functioning of JSNs.

iv. To identify the reading interests of the community and to compare with the reading materials available with the JSNs.

v. To prepare a profile of an effective prerak.

vi. To measure the attitude of preraks towards the various aspects of JSNs.

vii. To identify the problems faced by the preraks in organising the JSNs.

viii. To assess the community support received for the effective functioning of the JSNs.

In view of the above objectives, the following hypothesis were formulated for testing.

i. The availability of the proper infrastructure is likely to enhance the functioning of the JSNs.

ii. Positive attitude of the community towards the JSN is closely related with its effective functioning.

iii. The effective functioning of the JSNs depends on the availability of the suitable reading materials.

iv. Positive attitude of preraks towards various aspects of JSN leads to the effective functioning of JSNs.

v. Lesser the problems faced by the preraks in organising the JSNs higher will be the effective functioning of JSN.

vi. The effective functioning of the JSN depends on the degree of the support received from the community.

Methodology

For testing the above hypothesis certain data has to be collected from different sources. Hence the investigator has developed the tools viz a questionnaire on JSN performance, Community Attitude scale, Community Support Scale, Reading Interest Scale, Prerak Attitude Scale, Prerak Effectiveness Scale and Prerak Problems Scale.

The locale of the study was Rayalaseema region of Andhra Pradesh. Four hundred JSNs were functioning at the time of data collection in the region. For the purpose of the present study 100 JSNs were selected at random for choosing the various categories of sample. All the preraks working in these JSNs were formed as sample of the study. In addition five neo-literates and five community representatives were also chosen at random from each village representing the J.S.N. Thus a total of 100 preraks 500 neo-literates and 500 community representatives constituted the sample of the study.

The data was collected from the selected sample by administering the relevant tools to the selected sample by the investigator.

Before administering the tools a good report was established with the selected sample by explaining them the aim of the investigation and the way in which they have to respond to the items in the tools. The data thus collected were pool together and analysed by using suitable statistical techniques like Mean, SD., 't' test, chi-test and ANOVA etc.

The Major findings of the study

1. Majority of the JSNs were located in panchayath offices and at preraks residence. Most of the JSNs were functioned in the night for about one hour and are electrified. Almost all the JSNs have poor housing facilities and does not have adequates furniture and book keeping facilities.

2. The profile of the working preraks reveals that preraks belonging to Women, Forward Caste, Labour, More income, More experienced, More educated, Marrier, Elders, and belongs to more Positive Attitude groups were found to be more effective preraks.

3. The association between personal characteristics and effectiveness of the prerak discloses that caste of the prerak were found to be closely associated with their effectiveness.

4. The reading material supplied to the JSN and the reading interest of the neo-literates JSNs were found to be closely associated.

5. The study also reveals that prerak effectiveness also affects the JSNs performance. In otherwords, JSN's will be more effective if they were maned with effective preraks.

6. It is evident from the findings that there is a close association between the attitude possessed by the prerak and efficiency of the functioning of JSNs.

7. The JSNs manned by the preraks with moderate problems were found to be more effective than the preraks with more problems.

8. The JSNs with more community support were found to be more effective than the JSNs with less community support.

9. The performance of the JSNs were very effective wherever there is favourable attitude of the community towards various activities of the JSNs.

Suggestions for Future Research

1. Similar study can be undertaken with a large sample covering more aspects.

2. The performance of the JSN with special reference to a particular role can be conducted.

3. The impact of the various activities of the J.S.N. can be assessed on a particular group of sample.

4. Impact of the JSNs on retention of literacy can be undertaken.

BIBLIOGRAPHY

1. Adams (1964). *Measurement and Evaluation in Education, Psychology and Guidance*, New York: Holt Rinchrt and Winston Ink.

2. Adilakshmi (1993). *An investigation into the working conditions of the Jana Shikshana Nilayams and Opinion towards Jana Shikshana Nilayams,* Master Dissertation, S.P. Mahila University.

3. Directorate of Adult Education (1994). *A Report of the functioning of Jana Shikshan Nilayamas* 1993-94, New Delhi: Govt. of India.

4. Directorate of Adult Education. (1988). *Jana Shikshana Nilayam*, New Delhi: Govt. of India.

5. Directorate of Adult Education. (1988). *National Literacy Mission*: New Delhi: Govt. of India.

6. Janardhana Rao (1996). *An enquiry into the problems faced by the Monitors in Jana Chaitanya Kendras,* M.Phil Thesis, S.V. University.

7. Padmanabaiah and Kumarswamy (1995). "*An identification of the problems faced by the monitors*" Indian Journal of Adult Education Vol. 50(2) April-June pp. 42-46.

8. Ministry of Human Resource Development, (1986). *New Education Policy 1986: Programme of Action* New Delhi: Govt. of India.

9. Mohanty and Prusty (1996). *A Study of the Problems of functioning of Jana Shikshana Nilayams*" Indian Journal of Adult Education Vol. 57 (2) April-June pp. 46-51.

10. Muthuchamy (1992). *A Study of the Role Performance of the Preraks.* M.Phil Dissertation, Alagappa University.

11. Nair, Omanna and Rahim (1992). *A Study of the Programmes and Activities of JSN organised by Nehru Yuva Kendra in Kerala.* Trivandrum: Kerala Association for Non-formal Education and Development.

12. Reddeppa (1993). *A Study of the Determinants of prerak effectiveness*, M.Phil Thesis, S.V. University.

13. Shukla, A.N. (1972). *The concept of Extension Education: Study in Psychophysical Methods in PRS. Sinha (Ed.) Studies in Extension Education*, Hyderabad: National Institute of Community Development.

14. State Resource Centre (1995). *An observational study to identify the role of JSN in Continuing Education*, Mysore: SRC.

15. Vasumathi (1992). *A Study of the Organisation and Functions of Jana Shikshana Nilayams under Area Development Approach of the NLM in the Colleges of Kannur District*. Master Dissertation, Calicut University.

●●●

INDEX